THE INTERDEPENDENT WORLD
AND ITS PROBLEMS

KENNIKAT PRESS SCHOLARLY REPRINTS

Dr. Ralph Adams Brown, Senior Editor

Series on
ECONOMIC THOUGHT, HISTORY AND CHALLENGE
Under the General Editorial Supervision of
Dr. Sanford D. Gordon
Professor of Economics, State University of New York

THE
INTERDEPENDENT WORLD
AND ITS PROBLEMS

By

RAMSAY MUIR

KENNIKAT PRESS
Port Washington, N. Y./London

THE INTERDEPENDENT WORLD AND ITS PROBLEMS

First published in 1933
Reissued in 1971 by Kennikat Press
Library of Congress Catalog Card No: 76-137953
ISBN 0-8046-1455-5

Manufactured by Taylor Publishing Company   Dallas, Texas

KENNIKAT SERIES ON ECONOMIC THOUGHT,
HISTORY AND CHALLENGE

PREFACE

THIS little book is based upon some lectures given in the Universities of Leeds and Liverpool during the spring of 1932.

It is an attempt to bring out the profound political significance of the inspiring and terrifying world-crisis through which we are passing. Too few of us recognise that we are living in one of the most momentous periods of human history; and that the world may, in our lifetime, either pass into an era of secure peace and widely diffused prosperity, or be condemned to ruin and chaos, according as the governments of the world act wisely or foolishly. We have entered a new era, the era of world-interdependence; and this inter-dependent world is threatened with chaos because it has not learnt how to adjust its institutions and its traditions of government to the new conditions. This tremendous problem of adjustment is the theme which I have tried to discuss in a tentative and exploratory fashion.

Naturally I have had to deal with certain economic problems, since it is in the economic sphere that interdependence is most manifest. But I have discussed them only in a highly simplified —perhaps over-simplified—form, primarily as illustrations of the need for new world-institutions.

This little book contains no new or sensational facts, original theories, profound speculations, or magical remedies. It only attempts to put together familiar facts in such a way as may bring out their significance; and to draw the conclusions which (as I believe) those who think seriously about these facts can scarcely avoid drawing.

RAMSAY MUIR.

Richmond, Surrey,
November, 1932.

CONTENTS

CONTENTS

INTRODUCTION

FORTY years ago, when I was an undergraduate, I used to wish that my lot had fallen in an age, such as that of the Reformation or that of the French Revolution, when the destinies of mankind were being visibly changed by the course of events. If I had only known it, or if there had been anybody to tell me, I was living in just such an age; for the forces that have brought us into the remarkable new era which this little book attempts superficially to study were then very vigorously at work. I think all my studies in history, political science and economics would have taken on a greater vitality and a deeper significance if I had been enabled to realise the greatness of the problems of my own time.

But universities did not then, and perhaps do not now, regard it as any part of their duty to explain to the young student the problems of the world in which he is to live—at any rate in the sphere of politics. It is thought to be dangerous to touch upon controversial issues, and all the most vital issues in that field are controversial. So we studied the penetrating thought of Aristotle about the problems of the City-State of Ancient Greece, of Hobbes about the problems of sovereignty in the Nation-State of the seventeenth century weakened by civil strife, or of Rousseau about the dissolving monarchical and feudal order of the eighteenth century; and we were encouraged to apply to our own time generalisations suggested by totally different conditions. But nobody offered us any penetrating thought, or even challenged us to think for ourselves, about the tremendous problems created by the transition to a world-economy which was then taking place. Nobody, so far as I can remember, spoke or wrote about that at all; probably if anybody had, he would have been suspected of talking " hot air." We simply assumed that all the real problems of human organisation had been raised and settled in the distant past. It never dawned upon us that we were about to be faced with problems more complex and fundamental than any that Aristotle or Hobbes or Rousseau had considered: problems affecting not the organisation merely of a city, or of a Nation-State, or of a linked group of peoples such as those of Europe, but the organisation of a whole world, consisting of infinitely various peoples intimately linked together politically, culturally and economically.

To-day we have no excuse for shutting our eyes to these gigantic problems. The destiny of civilisation depends upon our capacity to deal with them. The thinking youth of to-day is conscious of being surrounded by immense and bewildering difficulties, and is honestly seeking for guidance. Unhappily we have no Aristotle, no Hobbes, no Rousseau to bring to bear upon them the force of a powerful and penetrating intelligence. We have to flounder

about as best we may, conscious of our own dis-
qualifications for dealing with a theme so vast, and
a little afraid of exposing them. I, most certainly,
have neither the breadth nor the piercingness of
vision that .would be necessary. for such an undertaking. Where a powerful searchlight is needed,
I can offer only a farthing dip. Yet even a farthing
dip may be better than no light at all; and here
it is.

CHAPTER I

It has become a platitude to say that the whole world is now interdependent. Men hear this said, in one form or another, from the platform or the pulpit, or read it in the leading articles of their newspapers, with no more sense of excitement than they feel when they hear or read that the world is round, or that there is a depression over Iceland.

Yet what a tremendous platitude it is! If all the peoples of the earth have been brought within a single social system; if no people can any longer be singly master of its own fate, but must depend for its security and prosperity upon the behaviour of the whole human family; and if this state of things is so well established that it is accepted as an obvious commonplace—then, surely, we have entered upon a new and thrilling era in human history, an era for which all the long millennia of man's troubled story have been a preparation. If this platitude is unalterably true, its implications must profoundly affect the conditions of human life for the future; it must transform all our thinking about social organisation; it must modify all our programmes and policies. Clearly we ought to be thinking seriously about it, and asking ourselves what it involves.

B

This is all the more necessary because the immense change involved in the establishment of world-interdependence has come about very rapidly, and without our realising, at all clearly, what was happening. When, in the light of what has happened, we look back over the course of history, we can see that the change has been in preparation during the last four centuries, ever since the European peoples began to extend their trade, their ideas and their methods of organisation over the rest of the world. But it only began to come rapidly in the nineteenth century. The pace was accelerated during the generation before the war; and since the war its effects have been so patent that in a very few years the fact of world-interdependence has become, as we have said, a mere platitude.

To analyse the significance and the consequences of this tremendous new stage in human development is the purpose of this little book. We must clearly begin by considering the actual facts of the situation as we see it to-day.

I. *The Conquest of Distance.*

Since time began, men have lived in more or less isolated communities, severed one from another, and prevented from understanding or influencing one another, by the difficulties of communication. It was impossible that diverse races, ignorant of each other's ideas, resources and ways of life, ignorant even of each other's existence, should grow together into a single social system, until distance was conquered and the transport of goods and the communication of knowledge were made easy.

The conquest of distance has been achieved very rapidly, mainly in the lifetime of men now living. Until a century ago, the speed at which we could communicate with one another over land or sea was limited by the pace of horses on ill-made roads, or of ships dependent upon the favours of the winds. Although relatively rapid progress had been made in the art of navigation since the fifteenth century, and all the seas of the world had been explored before the end of the eighteenth century, a long sea voyage was still in 1830 a very slow and tedious business, and the journey to China, Australia or Peru occupied many months, during which the traveller must be completely out of touch with the centres of civilisation. On land, progress in transport had been much less marked; and it may be doubted whether a traveller or a message could pass from Rome to Paris more rapidly at the end of the eighteenth century than in the prime of the Roman Empire. Dr. Johnson's tour in the Hebrides took more time, cost more money, inflicted greater discomforts on the traveller, and cut him off far more completely from all that was happening in his beloved London, than would a journey to the most distant regions of the earth to-day. When Warren Hastings was governor-general of India, the news of a disturbance in Delhi or Madras would take many days to reach him in Calcutta; six months or more might pass before the tidings reached the Directors of the East India Company in London, and yet another six months before their instructions could reach their representatives in India—by which time a war might have been fought

3

and lost or won. To-day the news of any event in the remotest part of India, or indeed anywhere on the face of the globe, may reach London within half-an-hour of its occurrence; and within another hour a squadron of aeroplanes, perhaps ordered from London, may be on swift flight to the scene of trouble, which it will reach in a few hours; or ships of war, plying the open sea, may receive through the ether orders to concentrate on a threatened point, speeding thither without regard to wind or tide at a pace vastly greater than our fathers ever thought possible.

This revolution in transport and communications, which has so amazingly knit together the whole world and brought its most distant points nearer to one another than London was to York a hundred years ago, has been wholly the work of the last century. First came the railway; and among the achievements of human labour there can have been none more gigantic than the enormous effort whereby a great part of the earth's surface has been woven together in three generations with a network of steel rails, piercing mountain barriers, tunnelling under or bridging over rivers, crossing deserts, and carrying over the face of the earth incredible loads of produce and incredible myriads of travellers. Then came the steamboat with its necessary apparatus of docks and wharves and loading apparatus on all the coasts of the world—another Herculean achievement. It has made the crossing of oceans less troublesome than a journey from London to Paris used to be; it has made the resources of the whole earth accessible to every region that can be reached from a port, taught all the peoples of the earth to use products they had never known, and almost banished the famine that used periodically to haunt many regions, by making the produce of the whole world available for their relief. The telegraph soon followed; and its wires and cables, less costly to lay than the steel roads of the railway, swiftly penetrated every part of the globe. These copper filaments have become, indeed, a sort of nervous system for the now unified world, flashing instantaneously to the great centres of affairs the news of whatever may be happening anywhere, as the nerves of the body instantly send word to the brain of whatever befalls foot or hand or eye or ear. Before the end of the century the telegraph was reinforced by its cousin the telephone, which carries over incredible distances the very tones of the human voice.

A fresh leap forward, and a still closer linking of the peoples of the earth, came with the early years of the twentieth century. The motor-car became in a few years the rival of the railway—not tied by steel rails or fixed times; able to go where no railway could go, and to carry on transport services where no railway could be remunerative, as across the Sahara or the deserts of Syria; and opening up undeveloped regions with less cost and greater speed than the railway could do. The conquest of the air was yet more rapid. Speeded by the needs of war, the aeroplane rapidly became a safe mode of transport, more swift than any other that man has yet created. Within a few years of the war, regular air-services for mails and passengers were spanning continents and seas, and reducing distances from weeks to days and from days to hours. The aeroplane makes nothing of frontiers; perhaps its future development will reduce tariffs and custom-houses to futility. Finally, wireless telegraphy, telephony and even television have (as it would seem) completed the conquest of distance, brought the most inaccessible places, including ships on the high seas, within reach of command, advice or warning from the nerve-centres of the world, and enabled a single human voice, speaking in London, New York or Moscow, to influence the thoughts of millions scattered over the face of the globe.

The annihilation of distance which has been brought about in all these ways is perhaps the most portentous revolution that has taken place in the course of human history. It has almost turned the whole world into a single city. Aristotle laid it down that no State should be so large as to make it impossible for all the citizens to hear the voices of their leaders speaking in the market-place: it is now almost possible for the whole human race to hearken to the actual voices of its leaders. Great empires have often broken up because the hand of power could not be quickly enough felt in their remoter regions: if there were a single lord of the earth to-day, his power could be more swiftly exhibited, anywhere from China to Peru, than Akbar's was from Agra to Benares.

The Great War gave many striking illustrations of the effects of this annihilation of distance. Austria issued an ultimatum to Serbia: within an hour every foreign office in the world was buzzing

with the fateful news. For eight days the statesmen of London, Paris, Berlin, Rome and St. Peters-
burg discussed with one another the possibilities of
avoiding war almost as freely as if they were in the
same city; while the statesmen of Ottawa, Canberra,
Pretoria, Wellington and Simla took counsel with
those of London. Then, after only eight days'
warning, armies so huge that they could not even
have been moved or fed in any earlier age, and
would have taken many months to get into position,
were crossing the frontiers on every side; while
other armies and navies were in motion in Asia
and Africa and on all the seas of the world. Because
distance had been annihilated and transport revolutionised, the most gigantic hosts in the history of
man were moved into action in a shorter time than
it took for a paltry local rising such as the Pilgrimage
of Grace to get itself into motion.

In peace as well as war, the annihilation of
distance has transformed the relations of men. It
has set myriads of travellers careering about the
world for pleasure, knowledge or trade; and is thus
rapidly breaking down the barriers between peoples.
Let a failure of the monsoon bring famine in a
district of India: instantly shiploads of food-stuffs
are ordered from the ends of the earth. Let an
unseasonable storm be reported in Texas: in a few
hours the price of cotton rises in Liverpool, Havre,
Bremen and Yokohama. Let the bank-rate rise or
fall one per cent. in London: immediately all the
money-markets of the world are affected. Let a
stock-exchange crash take place in New York:
next day the prices of securities fluctuate in every

stock-exchange in the world. The morning newspapers of the whole world contain items of intelligence from every corner of the earth—seldom well
selected, but nevertheless world-wide in their range.
A second-rate politician may have said, on the spur
of the moment, something piquant or indiscreet in
a speech at Aberdeen: next morning he will see
his indiscretion reported in every British newspaper,
and, before long, news-cuttings of his speech will
come to him from Peking, Madras, Adelaide,
Bloemfontein, Monte Video and Vancouver. The
whole earth has become a vast whispering gallery,
as fond of disconnected gossip as a village public-
house.

It is not possible to exaggerate the effects upon
world politics and upon economic life of this extraordinary revolution. In many respects, and for
many purposes, the world has shrunk to the size
of a market-town. Nothing has contributed more
to make the whole earth interdependent than the
conquest of distance which has been achieved
during the last century.

II. *The World a Single Political System.*

A second feature of the interdependence of the
modern world is that all the peoples of the earth
are now, whether consciously or not, members of
a single political system; in the sense that the political fortune of each of them is intimately linked
with the political fortunes of all the rest. Any
important event happening in any part of the earth
easily may, and probably will, involve the whole
world in its consequences. In June 1914 an

assassin fired a shot in the rude little town of Sarajevo, among the hills of Bosnia; and in a few weeks the whole world was wrapped in war, from Japan round the globe to the Falkland Islands. Unless the now unified world can effectively organise itself to prevent such consequences, another episode of the same kind might easily produce the same result: the recent trouble in Manchuria might have done so.

It is only recently that the whole world has been effectively brought within a single political system: until a century or two ago, the most violent political upheavals might take place in one region of the earth without traceably affecting the rest. Thus Asia, Africa, Australia and (for the most part) America were uninfluenced by the unending wars of Europe before the middle of the eighteenth century; and Europe felt no repercussions from the periodic dynastic wars and revolutions of India and China, or from the obscure warfare of Central Africa. It will never again be possible for any part of the world to be unaffected by the political troubles of any other part.

The main factor which has brought about this remarkable state of things has been the ebullient energy of the Nation-States of Europe, whose imperialist ambitions, during the last four centuries, have gradually brought the greater part of the world under their influence. Macaulay has noted, in picturesque phrases, how in the middle of the eighteenth century the outbreak of war in Europe set Red Indians tomahawking one another in the backwoods of America, and brought Indian princes into the field on the plains of the Ganges. That was an early stage in this secular process. In the nineteenth century it was carried much farther: Britain, France and Russia divided between them the greater part of the realm of Islam; and in the last quarter of the century there was a scramble among the European Powers for the possession of the last unoccupied territories of the earth, in Africa, south-eastern Asia and the Pacific, while Japan, having adopted the methods of the West, entered the competition, and China narrowly escaped partition. On the eve of the Great War, the whole world had been subjugated by Western civilisation; it was dominated by seven powerful empires, the British, the Russian, the French, the American, the German, the Italian and the Japanese; and the interests of these giants were so interlocked and interwoven in every part of the world that the perilous situation was created out of which the war sprang.

The Great War was itself the final proof that the whole world had been brought within a single political system, for every people on the face of the earth was directly or indirectly involved in it—even the Lamas of Tibet and the Samoyedes of Kamschatka. Amid all its horrors, the war had this august and tremendous aspect, that it was the first event in human history in which all the peoples of the earth were not only involved, but knew that they were involved. In his Chronicle of the First Crusade, Fulcher of Chartres has an eloquent passage in which he catalogues all the European peoples who gathered at Nicomedia before setting forth upon their march across Asia Minor, and triumphantly proclaims this evidence of the unity of Western Christendom. A catalogue of the races and tribes engaged in the Great War—even only of those who were in the long fighting lines, or in labour corps behind the lines—would provide a yet more striking testimony of the political unity of the world.

It was—it still is—a unity in disunity; a system of conflict, not yet a system of co-operation. In this it resembles the system of Ancient Greece, whose City-States were all alike affected by the great clash of the Peloponnesian war, yet all knew themselves to be parts of Hellas; it resembles the system of feudal Europe in Fulcher's time, a system of close interrelation but of incessant conflict; it resembles the system of the Nation-States of modern Europe, which, in the intervals of their unending wars, gathered in Congresses like those of Westphalia or Vienna to proclaim their adhesion to "the law of nations." The system of Ancient Greece collapsed in ruin, because it could not rise out of conflict into co-operation; the system of feudal Europe passed into that of national Europe, with its larger units; and this, in its turn, into the system of the World-States that dominated the world and swept it over the cataract of the Great War.

In the Great War, the world-system which had come insensibly into existence almost committed suicide. We are beginning to realise that any repetition of that disaster must mean the suicide of the civilisation which has brought some sort of unity within the reach of mankind. We are beginning to realise that, unless we can contrive to rise out of a system of conflict into a system of co-operation, a collapse like that of the Ancient Greek system, but far more fatal, and indeed irremediable, must ensue.

That is why the League of Nations was established as soon as the war was over—in an endeavour to save the world from collapse. Its establishment was not a mere piece of sentimentalism or unpractical idealism. It was a very practical necessity, recognised not by poets or dreamers, but by cynical men of affairs, who could not have made even their treaties of peace workable without the machinery thus set up.

However imperfect an instrument the League may be, and even if it should prove to be a total failure, its institution is a recognition of the established interdependence of the world; and it is a thrilling reflection for this generation that it has seen the establishment of the first organ ever created to serve the needs of the whole human race.

III. *Cultural Assimilation.*

Because the world has been closely linked by the conquest of distance, and because it has been brought within a single political system, a process of assimilation is steadily at work among its various peoples; their culture, their modes of life, their institutions become more like one another year by year. There are, of course, wide local and racial variations, which are preserved by national pride: long may they survive! But, in the main, the whole world is tending to adopt the fashions of the dominant West in most external things. At the same time other peoples are contributing something, and will perhaps contribute more and more, to the common civilisation of a unifying world: the arts of China and Japan, the philosophy of India, the barbaric music of Africa have their influence throughout the world.

It is in external things that this assimilation is perhaps most obvious. Everywhere men and women of the well-to-do classes wear clothes of the same styles, dictated by the arbiters of fashion in London and Paris. Almost everywhere the tables of the well-to-do are supplied with foods drawn from all over the globe, and cooked (more or less) according to the traditions of France. Almost everywhere the same games are played—nearly all of them derived from England. Football and lawn-tennis have become world-wide sports, in which nations compete with one another; so, in a less degree, have cricket and golf. All the peoples of the earth compete in the athletic sports, running, jumping, boxing, swimming; and these sports have their world-records and their world-championships. The institution, now nearly forty years old, of Olympic Games, open to the whole world and held in turn in different countries, is a token of world-unity, just as the original Olympic Games were a token of the unity of Ancient Greece. The bridge-table and the billiard-table compass the globe. Everywhere the gramophone reproduces the same music. Everywhere millions crowd the cinema-theatres; and the ways of life there held up to admiration and imitation, however vulgar they may be, possibly increase mutual understanding, and certainly lead to an increasing assimilation of manners. Finally, the wireless, infant as it is, must do more than almost any other factor to bring the world together. In almost every country men and women, by their own firesides, turn a switch and hear the songs or the speech of distant cities, or dance to the music of their bands.

Yet more important is the assimilation of the world's political systems and ideas: the whole world seems to have adopted the general ideas about human relationships and social organisation which were first developed in the countries of Western Europe. Almost everywhere slavery has been abolished, though it has been the foundation of human organisation throughout the greater part of the world since organised society began. Almost everywhere individual liberty of person, of speech, of thought, of belief and of association, under the protection of law, is claimed as an inherent and inalienable right, though it still has to face, in many countries, a difficult struggle against the traditions of caste and of inherited privilege. Almost everywhere the doctrine of the Reign of Law—the doctrine that no man's liberties may be impaired otherwise than by process of law—has been accepted; and Law is regarded no longer as the mere edict of supreme power, human or divine, but as the expression of the common will of the community. Almost everywhere the system of representative self-government working through parliamentary institutions has either been established or is clamantly demanded. Almost everywhere there has been an immense enlargement of the sphere of government, in response to the demand that the State shall provide for its citizens a multitude of services which they cannot adequately provide for themselves. The State is everywhere assuming responsibility for seeing that its subjects are not only protected against external attack and internal disorder, but are provided with the education which is necessary for the complexities of modern life, are afforded conditions of healthy life, and are safeguarded against abuses in the organisation of their labour. And everywhere these immense new functions are carried on by powerful bureaucracies. In short, the political methods of Western Europe, worked out slowly during the centuries of the modern age, are very rapidly becoming the political methods of the whole world.

The babel of diverse tongues still remains, what it has always been, the main obstacle to mutual understanding among the peoples of the earth; and it must continue to be so for the masses everywhere. But its effects are being qualified in various ways. The films speak a universal language, though their universality has been qualified since the introduction of the " talkies." The newspapers of all countries give news of all the world. Two or three languages —most notably English—are now so widely used that they have almost become world-tongues, and the educated in all lands are at least bilingual. It is (for an example) only by the common use of English that the diverse peoples of India, with their 138 distinct languages, have been able to act as in some degree a single community; and it may well be that in the future English may become what Latin was to mediæval Europe, for the various attempts that have been made to create an artificial world-language seem unlikely to lead to any considerable result.

In spite of the obstacles of diverse tongues, the world now possesses a common body of knowledge and thought, to which the peoples of all the developed countries make their contribution. Through translations, if not in the original, the principal writers of all countries are the common possession of the world, and address an audience no longer limited but world-wide. Science knows no frontiers; and the dazzling progress of knowledge in all fields, which has transformed within a century the conditions of human life and our outlook upon the universe, is not only a common possession of the world, but is the outcome of a vast co-operative enterprise in which the students and thinkers of many countries have shared.

This is equally true of the practical applications of science, which have during the last two generations given to mankind so amazing a control over the resources of nature that there is now no reason, other than human folly or mismanagement, why poverty or overwork should any longer exist in the world.

This control has been won by the invention of elaborate mechanism for every purpose of production and distribution, by the harnessing to mechanism of power derived from new sources, and by the organisation of flexible methods of finance whereby, through the canalising of innumerable rivulets of private thrift, the means have been found for gigantic undertakings such as no previous generation of mankind could have envisaged. In the development of mechanism, of power, and of financial methods the inventors of many countries have

16

shared, though the lead in each case came from England. But in the enjoyment of the fruits of these new instruments of productive power, all countries alike have shared. Mechanism, power and joint-stock finance are the common possessions of the unified world. In varying degrees, every region of the world is being industrialised—that is to say, is learning to use mechanism, power and finance to wrest from nature a more abundant provision for the needs of man; and the conditions of human life are everywhere being transformed with a speed that increases with each generation.

In short, the world has not only been brought together by the conquest of distance, and included within a single political system, it now shares a single civilisation, whose pressure assimilates its people progressively to one another.

IV *Economic Interdependence.*

The most impressive and the most fundamental aspect of the world's interdependence is in the economic sphere.

It is not long since every little tribe or village community was practically self-sufficient in an economic sense, and capable of carrying on almost its normal life if the rest of the world had been submerged. As late as the eighteenth century countries such as France and England were substantially self-sufficient: they drew from beyond their own borders only inessential luxuries; and the normal life of the mass of their people would have been almost undisturbed if the rest of the world had been destroyed. To-day there is no country or empire, however great and however rich in natural resources, whose normal modes of life are not dependent upon supplies of goods drawn from every part of the world.

One of the most striking illustrations of our growing interdependence is to be found in the rapidity with which the civilised world has become dependent upon tropical produce derived from regions which were practically unknown, and wholly unexploited, fifty or a hundred years ago. What should we do without the rubber, the vegetable oils, the cocoa, and so forth, which come to us out of tropical Africa and Malaysia? We could exist, no doubt; but we should be deprived of some of the things that have come to seem normal elements in our daily life.

The first country to realise her dependence upon the rest of the world was England. As early as 1773 she found that she could no longer feed her people with the produce of her own soil, and she has never since been able to do so; and during the following generation her most thriving industry came to be one which had to draw the whole of its raw materials from the other side of the Atlantic—the cotton industry. As early as 1776 a great British thinker, Adam Smith, revolutionised economic science by working out the theory of interdependence. He showed that the chief source of human wealth was the division of labour and the free interchange of the products of specialised work; he showed that the division of labour operated, and ought to be allowed to operate freely, not only between man and man, or between one district and another in the same country, but between one country and another;

and, finally, he showed that the well-being not only of an individual country but of the whole world could best be forwarded by encouraging this division of labour and permitting the free interchange of its products. He thus set forth the philosophy of an economically interdependent world before the fact of interdependence had even begun to be apparent. During the nineteenth century Britain, alone among the great countries of the world, accepted the fact of interdependence, made it the foundation of her policy, and by adopting the doctrine of Smith and his successors, made herself the pivot and centre of the world's economic system. She adopted this policy before the interdependence of the world had been established. She has abandoned it at the moment when the economic interdependence of the world has become the controlling factor in the world's affairs.

Many nations to-day are endeavouring to shut their eyes to the fact of economic interdependence, and are still pursuing a self-sufficiency which is utterly unattainable. This is the main cause of the troubles from which the world has been suffering since the war, and which we shall have to examine in a later chapter.

In the United States of America, for example, President Hoover has stated that his great country can recover from her troubles by her own strength, because she is self-sufficient and need not concern herself about the distresses of the world. Yet ten or twelve million workers are unemployed in the United States, her banks have been failing by scores, and some of her cities are bankrupt, because she cannot sell to the rest of the world the goods with which her warehouses are bursting. No doubt it is true that if the rest of the world were suddenly destroyed the United States could provide her people with a generous subsistence. But her whole economic system would have to be painfully reorganised before she could do so; and she could not provide them with many of the things which have come to appear essential in modern life. She could not give them tea, coffee or cocoa, or more than a very inadequate supply of sugar. She could not give them the enormous newspapers they demand, or anything like the amount of artificial silk they now use, because she has so wasted her forests that she cannot now satisfy her own requirements in timber. Her people would have to do without rubber-tyred automobiles and rubber-floored bathrooms. It has been asserted that she could not make for them any aeroplanes, electric lamps, or wireless sets, because some of the essentials for these products come from abroad. She could not produce many of the modern types of steel, and steel is one of the most essential materials of modern civilisation: over forty of the requisites for modern steels are imported by her from as many different countries—nickel from Canada, vanadium from the High Andes of Peru, or chromium from New Caledonia, for examples. The needs of war would not concern her if the rest of the world had been blotted out; but, as that happy event has not yet taken place, it is worth noting that the American war department has listed thirty substances, essential to modern warfare, which she either does not produce at all, or produces in insufficient quantities. Not even the United States can be self-sufficient in the modern world. She has to buy many things from the rest of the world if her people are to live the sort of life to which they are accustomed; she has to sell vast quantities of raw materials and manufactured goods to the rest of the world if her people are to be kept in employment.

France also considers herself to be economically self-sufficient; and no doubt she could feed, clothe and house all her people even if she were cut off from the rest of the world. But the whole texture of their lives would be changed. This is well brought out in a passage in which M. Francis Delaisi describes a day in the life of a French middle-class business man; I make no apology for quoting it, because it is largely applicable to every other European country.

" M. Durand begins his day by washing himself with soap made from Congo nuts, and drying himself with a towel made in Lancashire from cotton grown in Texas. He puts on a shirt and collar of Russian linen, a suit made of wool from Australia or the Cape, a silk tie woven from Japanese cocoons, and shoes whose leather came from an Argentine ox, and has been tanned with German chemicals. In his dining-room, which is adorned with a Dutch sideboard made of wood from Hungarian forests, the table is furnished with spoons and forks of plated metal, made of Rio Tinto copper, tin from the Straits, and Australian silver. His fresh loaf is of wheat from the Beauce, Rumania or Canada, according to the season; he has a slice of chilled lamb from the Argentine, with tinned peas from California; his sweet includes English jam made of French fruit and

Cuba sugar, and his excellent coffee comes from Brazil. He goes to his office in an American car; and after noting the quotations of the Liverpool, London, Amsterdam and Yokohama exchanges, he dictates his correspondence, which is taken down on an English typewriter, and signed with an American fountain-pen. In his factory fancy goods for Brazilian customers are being manufactured of materials of many origins, by machinery made in Lorraine on a German patent, and fed with English coal: he gives instructions that they are to be sent to Rio by the first German boat sailing from Cherbourg. He then goes to his bank, to pay in a cheque in guilders from a Dutch client, and to buy sterling to pay for English goods. After a profitable day, he proposes to spend the evening at a show with his wife. She dons her blue fox fur from Siberia, and her diamonds from the Cape; they dine in an Italian restaurant, go to see the Russian ballet, and after supper at a Caucasian cabaret to the music of a negro jazz band, they return home. As M. Durand falls asleep under his quilt of Norwegian duck-feathers, he thinks with pride of the greatness of France, entirely self-supporting and able to snap her fingers at the whole world ! "

A yet more striking demonstration of the extent to which interdependence has been carried is afforded by the transformation which has taken place in the life of the primitive peoples. The tribes of negro Africa, many of which had never seen a white man until Livingstone or Stanley visited them fifty or sixty years ago, had lived contentedly since time was young on the produce of their tribal lands.

Now they are engaged in producing vegetable oils for the soap-vats of Port Sunlight, rubber for the motor-factories of Detroit and Coventry, or cocoa for the chocolate works of Switzerland and Bournville. And they spend the income thus derived on cotton goods from Lancashire made of fibres from America, India or Egypt, or on gay blankets made in Belgium from the waste of Australian wool; they roof their huts with corrugated iron made in South Wales of Belgian steel; and they eat canned foods from America, getting access to them with German tin-openers. The very foundations of their life have been revolutionised; having lived apart for centuries in complete self-sufficiency, they find themselves dependent for their livelihood upon remote countries of which they know almost nothing.

In short, all the peoples of the world have become inextricably bound up with all the other peoples of the world. Their very livelihood depends, in a greater or less degree, upon the incessant interchange of goods and services, and the whole world has become a single complex economic organism. It can be ruined by any interruption of the process of interchange upon which its life depends; and the consequences may be equally serious whether this interruption is caused by the crude brutality of war or by the subtler peril of economic mismanagement or maladjustment. No nation however great can any longer safeguard itself against these dangers by its own strength alone; the well-being of each now depends ineluctably upon the well-being of all.

Nor does this complete the picture of economic interdependence. The greatest productive under-

takings are now no longer confined within a single
country; their activities extend over the world.
Consider how the production of mineral oil is
organised: it has in half a century become one of
the substances most vital to civilised life. It is in
the hands of a few gigantic corporations, which own
nearly all the oil fields of the world, and supply
almost all the needs of the world: they have their
head-offices in America or London or Amsterdam,
but they are essentially world-concerns, not national
concerns. Consider, again, such an undertaking
as Unilevers, which has its main centres in England
and Holland, but owns innumerable factories in
England and in half the countries of the world, and
copra-yielding islands in the Pacific, and vast
estates in Africa. These giants are not merely
national undertakings. During the last generation
concerns of this type, which disregard national
frontiers, or consider them as mere impediments,
have been becoming more numerous and more
important. And alongside of them there have grown
up, especially since the war, great international
cartels or combines, which attempt to regulate or
control whole lines of trade. They are not effectively
subject to the company or commercial law of any
single country; and if their formidable activities
are to be regulated at all, it must be by some international authority, such as does not yet exist.

Finally, there is coming about a very remarkable
diffusion of the ownership of many of the world's
productive activities among the peoples of the world.
Property, since the invention of the joint-stock
company, has assumed a new form. It no longer

consists solely of the direct ownership of land or chattels, tangible things, but of claims to a share in the profits of various concerns, these claims being represented by documents which can be readily bought and sold. The list of stock-exchange transactions in any issue of *The Times* shows the freedom with which these titles to a share in the profits of undertakings in every part of the world are transferred from one owner to another, and how wide is the range of the interests thus involved. A yet wider diffusion of ownership rights is implied in the creation of Investment Trust Companies, which have been increasing rapidly in number in recent years. When a small investor puts £100 into an Investment Trust, he does not acquire any tangible property; he acquires a claim to a minute share of the yield from a multitude of ownership-rights distributed over the world. This country has taken the lead in the acquisition of these ownership-claims in other countries; but the practice is growing, and (if prosperity returns) is likely to grow rapidly; and we may anticipate a future in which the rights of ownership in the productive activities of the world will be distributed among all the peoples of the world; and in which even the small investor will draw his income, not from one identifiable farm or factory, but from the general industrial and trading activity of the world.

V. *Britain's Place in the Interdependent World.*

It is but a cursory and generalised survey of our interdependent world that we have taken in this chapter; but it is perhaps sufficient to show how profound, many-sided and far-reaching are the changes which the developments of the last century have brought about in the relationships of the earth's peoples. The world has been knit together by the conquest of distance. It has been welded into a single political system. It is more and more dominated by a single civilisation or culture, so that almost every part of it uses the same dress, plays the same games, shares a common body of knowledge, uses or aspires after the same political institutions and ideas, and employs the same methods of producing and distributing wealth. The very livelihood of each member of this interdependent world now depends upon contributions drawn from all the other members; and both the conduct and the ownership of productive enterprise are increasingly assuming a world-wide scale. Here, certainly, is a revolution more momentous than humanity has ever experienced in its history: here is the opening of an exciting new era in human history.

It is natural that an Englishman should be tempted to dwell upon the great part which his country has played in this momentous revolution. Britain has taken the giant's share in the conquest of the world by Western civilisation, from which the world's nascent political unity has sprung. She initiated some of the most important among the new methods of transport and communication which have linked the world together. From her came the beginnings of the industrialism which has transformed the condition of human life—the development of machinery, the use of new kinds of power, the working out of the elastic methods of modern finance. She gave to the world the games and sports which most of its peoples now play. Her hospitable and flexible language is the most widely spoken in the world, and stands a better chance than any other of becoming the principal common tongue of a unified world. She was the first country to attain to the powerful and stable organisation of the Nation-State, the first to achieve the reality of personal liberty under the shelter of the reign of law, and the inventor of the system of parliamentary government. She was the first nation to recognise her economic dependence upon the rest of the world, and that dependence is in her case more absolute and obvious than in the case of any other country. She was, during the critical period when interdependence was being established, the very pivot of the world's economic system, its central market, its chief carrier, its financier, its money-lender, and the manipulator of its monetary system; and during the years of her ascendancy there was no such grave dislocation as we have seen in recent years. In short Britain has been, in a very remarkable degree, the source of most of the factors which have contributed to produce the interdependent world of to-day.

This imposes upon her a very heavy responsibility, which is deepened by the fact that her very existence depends upon the successful functioning of the interdependent world. More than any other nation, she is called upon to realise the immense potential advantages that can be derived from interdependence, and the terrible dangers that attend it. The peace and well-being of every people now depend upon the peace and well-being of the world as a whole. If the interdependence of all peoples can be rightly

27

used, it can bring an unimagined prosperity to the whole human race; for we have reached that culminating moment in human history in which Man has achieved such a mastery over Nature that nothing save his own misguided folly prevents him from banishing war and poverty and unending drudgery from the earth—the ills which have attended all his long upward struggle. On the other hand, if interdependence is not rightly understood and used, it threatens a ruin more terrible than could ever have befallen mankind in the days of isolated and self-sufficient social units. The peoples of the earth are like climbers roped together on a rock-face, struggling to reach a summit from which a glorious vista will be revealed. If any of them start playing the fool, or acting as if the rope did not exist, the whole train may be precipitated into the abyss; and at this moment most of them seem bent upon playing the fool and scrambling into the nearest crevice for safety, without considering what strains this will impose upon the rope, above them and below them, and what dangers to themselves as well as to their fellow-climbers.

We shall in later chapters attempt to discuss more fully the perils and the necessary consequences of interdependence. But first it is necessary to look more closely at some of the causes which have helped to bring this state of interdependence into existence, and, in particular, at the political factors involved; because these, and especially the spirit of nationalism, are of such a kind as to intensify most seriously the already difficult problems which face the world.

CHAPTER II

NATIONALITY AND INTERDEPENDENCE

If we are to understand the significance of the condition of world-interdependence which we surveyed in the last chapter, it is necessary to appreciate the factors which have brought it about; and, in particular, the potent spirit of nationalism, which has been the most powerful political factor in the life of the world during the last four centuries, and is perhaps more powerful to-day than it has ever been. This was the driving-force which impelled the Nation-States of Western Europe to bring the whole world under the influence of Western civilisation, and thus to bring it within a single political system.

It may be said that economic rather than political factors—industrialism, joint-stock finance, the creation of new modes of transport and communication—have mainly contributed to make the whole world interdependent; and this is undoubtedly true. But all the economic developments which have transformed the world originated in the Nation-States of Western Europe and America, and it was their devouring energy and their irresistible strength which extended them throughout the world. Why was this? It was because the Nation-States gave to their citizens freedom for initiative and experiment;

because they afforded to the undertakings inspired by this freedom the protection of strong government and firmly administered law; and because they were strong enough to extend this protection to the adventurous enterprises of their citizens in every part of the world. In the last analysis, the achievements of the European peoples were made possible by their political system, which had found a cement strong enough to bind together great aggregates of people in a common loyalty. The spirit of nationalism, which has been the most potent factor in the shaping of the modern world, can be, like fire, a very powerful civilising force; but it can also be, like fire when it is out of control, a very dangerous destructive force. It is therefore indispensable that we should study the achievements, the virtues and the perils of this potent spirit.

We may perhaps distinguish three broad eras in the history of human organisation: first, an era of small self-sufficient units, cemented by the loyalty of neighbourhood, and sometimes brought under the military ascendancy of evanescent empires; secondly, an era of firmly organised national States, cemented by the loyalty of patriotism; and thirdly, the era, now beginning, of world economy, for which no adequate cement has yet been discovered. The transition from the first era to the second was slow, toilsome, and only partial. The transition from the second era to the third, which has been forced upon us by the rapid development of interdependence, cannot but be attended by many difficulties and dangers, and presents political problems more perplexing than men have ever had to face before. But a study of the difficulties that attended the first transition may perhaps help us to understand those of the second.

I. *The Era of Small Social Units.*

Over the greater part of the earth's surface, and during almost the whole of human history, the normal grouping of men has been in small local units, united by the cement of kinship (real or supposed), or of mere neighbourhood. Such units have been tribes or clans, village communities, City-States, feudal baronies, market-town districts. They have mostly been almost or wholly self-sufficient; for that reason they have largely lived in isolation, and have been suspicious of neighbouring communities; and they have therefore frequently been at war

The existence of great empires wielding power over wide territories, such as the Babylonian, the Assyrian, the Persian, the successive empires that rose and fell in India, or the Ottoman empire, has not in fact seriously invalidated the truth of this generalisation, because these empires have mostly been little more than tribute-collecting military ascendancies, which did not materially affect the normal life of the small self-contained units included within them. They have nearly always been short-lived, because they were not cemented by anything stronger than common subjection to the will of a master, and therefore could not command the lasting loyalty of their subjects. Even religious enthusiasm, which created the first Mohammedan empire, was not by itself enough to hold it together.

31

The empires, such as the Roman and the Chinese, which have succeeded in impressing upon their subjects a distinctive civilisation have been few indeed; and it is true that the normal group of men which was able to hold together because it could command the loyalty of its members has always, until a recent epoch, been a small local group, whose members could personally know one another.

These small tribal, village, city or feudal units were normally self-sufficient in an economic sense. An English village in the eleventh century, for example, produced from its own fields all the food the villagers ate, the hides or homespun with which they clothed themselves, the stone, clay, wattles, timber and thatch of which their huts were made; and needed to draw nothing from beyond its own limits save iron and salt and the superfluous luxuries of its masters. These small social units were suspicious of one another: whether tribes, City-States or feudal baronies, they were easily embroiled in local wars. They regarded " foreigners " from other tribes or cities with distrust, and if they came to trade, hampered them with dues and other restrictions. It was not easy for almost self-sufficient groups to regard trade as an interchange of benefits; they thought of the foreign trader not as offering to them a wider range of satisfactions, but as taking the bread out of the mouths of their own people—as a dangerous fellow, who ought not to be encouraged. Like other primitive and ancestral fears and prejudices, this distrust of the unscrupulous foreigner and his goods survives, or is easily awakened, even among comparatively civilised people. These defects of the self-sufficient small social units had to be overcome before man could make any effective progress towards peace or material well-being: some higher force, some wider loyalty, had to put an end to local wars, and to demolish the local barriers to trade.

The transition to larger units, rendering possible a richer and more varied life, was not easy. In actual fact, it was scarcely ever achieved except by force. Wars of conquest, like slavery, were, indeed, in the earlier stages of man's development, necessary to his progress. Without forced labour, it may be doubted whether man would have made the transition from the free life of the hunter and the nomad to the steady drudgery of the cultivator; and it was the leisured class which slavery made possible that invented fresh wants and created the arts. Without wars of conquest, larger units than the self-sufficient districts we have been discussing would not have come into existence—at any rate they did not come into existence by any other means. Will anyone aver that the wars which turned the Heptarchy into the Realm of England were not beneficial to the world? Will anyone who realises what the Roman Empire did for Western civilisation question the value of the wars which created it, cruel and wicked as many of them were? War, like slavery, was a necessary instrument of human progress during many long ages. It ceased to be a necessary instrument, and became purely an evil, when the interdependence of mankind had been brought to such a point that war could only dislocate and devastate, but could yield no fruitful results. Like slavery, its evilness

D   33

only became apparent when it had ceased to serve any useful constructive purpose.

But the creation of larger political units by conquest could not lead to any permanent results, as the history of a hundred evanescent empires has shown, unless there could be created in these larger units a loyalty strong enough to overcome the obstinate loyalties of kinship and neighbourhood which were the strength of the little local units; a loyalty strong enough to forbid local wars and to sweep aside local tariffs or other obstacles to trade and intercourse. None of the empires of history ever succeeded in evoking such a loyalty to serve as cement for its subjects, not even the empires of Rome and China. The secret of the great achievements of the Western European peoples is that, unconsciously, they discovered, in the loyalty of nationality, the cement which could bind together great masses of men and wide territories in a lasting unity This alone enabled them to create great States so strong that they could give to their subjects the freedom of thought, investigation and experiment out of which progress comes; so well obeyed that there was within them full security for enterprise under the protection of law; and so powerful that they could uphold and protect their citizens in all their adventures in every part of the world. In short, the development of the national State was one of the most momentous advances in human history; and it has made posssible all the progress of the last few centuries.

II. *The Growth of Nationalism and its Achievements.*

The doctrine of nationality—the doctrine that every nation, because it is a nation, ought to be organised as a separate State—has become so much a part of our ordinary habits of thought that most of us accept it as an axiom; we seldom realise that the idea of nationality has only played a part in human affairs in comparatively recent times; and we scarcely ever ask ourselves what we mean by the word " nation."

A nation may perhaps be defined as a body of people who believe that they " belong together," because they are united by ties of national affinity so strong that it is painful to them either to be politically divided, or to be subjected to any external power which they can regard as alien.

It is not easy to define with any precision the natural affinities which are necessary to constitute nationhood. The occupation of a clearly defined territory; a sense of racial unity (which is usually imaginary, since all peoples are of mixed race), or at least the absence of any sharply felt racial cleavages; the possession of a common language, especially if it has become the vehicle of a great literature; common standards of conduct; long habitual obedience to the same body of law or custom, and observance of the same social usages; great traditions of triumphs enjoyed and sufferings endured in common—all these factors can powerfully contribute to inspire a strong national sentiment, and to weld a people into unity. There have been instances in which a real national unity has been

35

established in the absence of one or more of these factors; but most of them must be present before the claim to nationhood can be effectively made good, or stand the strain of internal differences and external pressure.

The national spirit is stimulated quite as much by a sense of difference from other nations as by a sense of unity within the nation itself; and for this reason nationalism tends to encourage conflict. Once a nation has established its unity and freedom, it is always tempted to impose its power upon other less unified peoples; and when it does so, it often stimulates the national spirit among these also. It is, in fact, to this cause that the extension of the national idea throughout the world is mainly due; and it is this spirit of national pride which has driven the nations of Europe forward to the conquest of the world.

The national idea had its birth and early development in Western Europe, and it is only in recent years that its influence has been extended beyond Europe —partly in imitation, partly in protest against the domination of the European peoples. We may usefully distinguish four stages in its development.

The first stage was marked by the gradual and unconscious emergence of the system in Western Europe during the later Middle Ages. England was the first country in the world to achieve national unity, and to be stimulated by the consciousness of its nationhood. This achievement can be dated in the thirteenth century; and its first result was that the English, in the pride of their nationhood, strove to impose their power upon their more divided neighbours in Wales, Ireland, Scotland and France. The immediate consequence was the creation of a powerful spirit of nationality in these countries also; and Scotland and France were the second and third nations to assert their national unity and freedom. Spain and Portugal, after their long struggle against the Moors, Holland in the course of her resistance to the might of Spain, and Sweden after a struggle to escape from control by the Poles, next took their places in the ranks of the Nation-States; and by the sixteenth century a group of Nation-States, the first in the world, extended along the Atlantic coast of Europe from north to south.

The second stage occupied the modern age from the sixteenth century to the nineteenth, and demonstrated the strength and vigour of the national type of State. The history of these centuries was completely dominated by the rivalries of the new Nation-States, and by their eagerness to expand their power. They seldom attempted to conquer one another's national territory, and never succeeded in doing so; for nations once united can display a formidable strength in defending the sacred territory, as Spain showed in the Spanish Succession War, Holland when she was attacked by the might of Louis XIV, and France when all the monarchies invaded her soil in 1793: the boundaries of the Nation-States, once fixed, have shown an extraordinary permanence. The rivalries of the nations were fought out in two kinds of areas where they saw opportunities of extending their power—in the "unnationalised" region of Europe, including Germany and Italy; and in the non-European

37

world—the new world beyond the Atlantic and the old world of Asia.

Beyond question, the immense energy displayed during the sixteenth, seventeenth and eighteenth centuries in the colonisation of North and South America, and in the extension of European trade and power in India and Malaysia, was due to the pride, strength and energy of the Nation-States. The proof of this is that only the Nation-States succeeded in creating over-sea empires—Spain, Portugal, England, Holland and France: the Germans and the Italians, though they had shown themselves in the Middle Ages to be the best traders and navigators of Europe, and were well fitted to play the part of settlers in new lands, had no share in this immense movement because they lacked the stimulus and support of a national organisation.

Moreover, it was the national spirit which held these scattered empires together. In the chaos of eighteenth-century India, for example, the Mogul's satraps, or soldiers of fortune such as Hyder Ali, could carve out personal dominions for themselves, because, lacking the sense of nationality, they had no feelings of patriotism. What they did, a Dupleix or a Clive, a Bussy or a Hastings could easily have done; and if the Corsican Bonaparte, who had no strong national feeling, had found his way to India (as he longed to do) he would assuredly have created, not a French or a British, but a Napoleonic empire. It never occurred to Dupleix or Clive, Bussy or Hastings, to use their opportunities for the creation of personal sovereignties—not because they were too scrupulous or too timid, but because national feeling was in them so strong that it interested them far more to create great dominions for England and for France; and even the grossest ingratitude was not strong enough to overcome this sentiment. What is true of India is true also of other distant lands. Nothing less powerful than the national spirit could have held together the widely scattered dominions created by the European Nation-States.

The potency of nationalism was thus very fully demonstrated during the sixteenth, seventeenth and eighteenth centuries; a new power had come into human life. But it had never been analysed or deliberately fomented; it had just come into existence where the circumstances were favourable. In the nineteenth century what may be called the *doctrine* of nationality began to be preached—the doctrine that nationality is the only just foundation of state-hood, and that the limits of States ought always to be determined, not by the accidents of conquest or dynastic inheritance, but by the natural affinities of peoples. The great apostle of this doctrine was Mazzini; he had disciples in many lands; and the growing demands of divided nations for union, and of subject nations for freedom, became (along with the kindred demand for the rights of self-government) the chief disturbing factor, on the political side, throughout the nineteenth century.

Two great victories were won for the national cause when Germany and Italy, whose weakness in division had made them for three centuries the helpless victims of the consolidated Nation-States, achieved their unity. At once they took their place among the Great Powers; they made rapid progress in the industrial arts, in which they had been left far behind; and they claimed their " place in the sun," their share in the control of the non-European world, all the more vigorously because they had started so late in the race. In accordance with the universal rule that the pride of achieved nationhood drives triumphant nations to assert themselves without much regard to their neighbours, Germany and (in a less degree) Italy became aggressive and disturbing elements in the life of Europe and the world, as England, Spain and France had earlier been; and this natural assertiveness was one of the main provoking causes of the Great War.

Several of the little nations of south-eastern Europe—Greece, Rumania, Serbia and Bulgaria—also obtained during the nineteenth century a partial satisfaction of their national aspirations, but only enough to stimulate them to further ambitions, so that they also became centres of the unrest that preceded the Great War. Elsewhere—in the Austrian Empire, in Poland and in the western part of the Russian Empire—the ferment of nationalism was busily at work. Nationalism had thrown most of Europe into a fever, which could only be allayed by the satisfaction of these aspirations, and by a recast of the political map on the lines dictated by the natural affinities of peoples, and no longer on the lines defined by ancient conquests or by dynastic inheritance. This fever created the conditions out of which the war came; and when the war was over, an attempt was made deliberately to reconstruct the whole of Europe on national lines. Thus, within the century between 1815 and 1919, the *doctrine* of nationality had been not only formulated but carried into effect for Europe. It had been accepted as a principle of Western civilisation that— at any rate in Europe—nationality and the natural affinities of peoples constitute the only sound and defensible basis for the organisation of States.

Meanwhile the fourth stage in the development of the national system—its extension from Europe to the non-European world—had already begun. Its beginnings may be dated about 1880, when the Indian National Congress was established, and when a nationalist ferment in Egypt brought about the rising of Arabi Pasha. Since that date, and with accelerating rapidity since the Great War, the nationalist fever has spread throughout a great part of the world. It has been stimulated by the emphasis laid upon " self-determination," which was defined by President Wilson as essential to the peaceful settlement of the world. The phrase covers both the idea of national freedom and the idea of self-government, both of which have come to be regarded as necessary elements in the organised life of a civilised State. But it is a dangerous phrase, because it obscures the fact that in an interdependent world no man and no nation can be trusted to determine his or its own destiny without reference to the claims of other individuals and other nations. Catchwords and formulæ, however, have a very powerful influence upon the minds of men; and the catchword of " self-determination " has played an important part in shaping the course of events and the movement of ideas since the war.

The extension of the national spirit over the world

has been shown in the modern attitude of the British Dominions, which has (so far as the Dominions are concerned) reduced the British Empire to be the loosest political group that has ever existed: it is looser than even the world-wide League of Nations, for its members undertake no specific obligations, and have no regular machinery for consultation and joint action. Nationalism has thrown India into a ferment, and created in that vast land a political problem of the greatest complexity and difficulty. It has reduced China almost to chaos, and exposed her as an almost helpless victim to the ambitions of Japan: but it is possible that the Japanese attack may (in the manner so often reproduced in the history of the national principle) actually consolidate the disorganised empire by intensifying the national feeling which has hitherto been largely artificial. Nationalism has transformed the world of Islam since the war, destroying the theocratic unity to which the Moslem peoples have always clung, in theory if not in practice, just as it destroyed the unity of Latin Christendom in the Middle Ages. The nationalist ferment is actively at work in Turkey, in Syria, in Iraq, in Arabia, in Palestine (where it is creating a very difficult relationship between the resident Arabs and the immigrant Jews), and even in Morocco. Its influence may yet extend to the backward peoples of Africa, and throw that continent, just beginning to emerge from barbarism, into a new confusion. Finally, the nationalist aspiration is having a disruptive effect even in some of the European countries where it might seem to have been given a reasonable satisfaction. It has severed

Norway from Sweden. It has produced friction between the Flemings and the Walloons in Belgium. It has created the Irish Free State. It has stimulated a demand for autonomy in Catalonia. It has set the Croats and the Serbs of the new State of Jugo-Slavia, and the Czechs and Slovaks of the new State of Czecho-Slovakia, at issue with one another. In short, after having proved itself a powerful constructive force, cementing men into larger political units, and impelling these larger units forward to the unification of the world, it is now showing itself also as a disruptive force, asserting the need for organisation in smaller units.

Dangerous as it is to make confident predictions in a rapidly changing world, it would seem that the national State has now become the accepted form of political organisation, and that the predominant units in the interdependent world of the future will be Nation-States. There are dangers in this development. But there are also very good reasons for satisfaction that the State-units of the world tend to be societies that are cemented by the natural affinities of their citizens, and not merely held together in an enforced obedience to the will of a master.

III. *The Virtues of Nationalism.*

The secret of the strength of national States is that they have been able to evoke among their subjects a loyalty more intense, even more passionate, than any other form of State—unless we make an exception for the City-States of the ancient world—has ever been able to evoke. The emotion of patriotism may

43

seem to rarefied intelligences almost irrational; but it is a fact, not to be denied, a factor in the life of civilised societies which cannot be left out of account, and which stultifies all anticipations that are based upon mere calculations of self-interest. The patriot, like the martyr, makes the " economic man " look, not perhaps foolish, but anæmic. " My country, right or wrong," may be ethically unsound; but it represents the operative conviction, the living faith, of millions of commonplace people, to whom the call of country counts for more than self-interest, or family, or career, or life itself. No one who saw, during the early years of the Great War, the readiness with which exiled citizens of the belligerent nations abandoned their careers and voluntarily crossed the seas at their own expense in order to offer themselves as sacrifices on the altars of their countries can ever question the overmastering power of this emotion. The prophecies, freely made before the war, that " the workers " would refuse to be butchered at the command of their " masters," were stultified in every country. Prophecies are now often made as to the impossibility of bringing out the manhood of the nations for another war; but if the test came, these prophecies would no doubt be as completely falsified as their predecessors.

This master-passion, however mysterious its sources, is no doubt most powerfully stirred, as many historical examples show, when the sacred soil of the homeland is threatened by invasion; and yet " the homeland " can be no more than an abstraction to the denizens of city slums or the drudges of the fields. But this sentiment gives an extraordinary sacredness and permanence to national boundaries, once they are established, such as the boundaries of dynastic States could never possess: and it therefore promises a stability in a world of Nation-States such as a world consisting of units of a different type could not hope to attain.

In this passion, the States of the modern world have found a social cement more binding than any other human societies which have existed on the earth have known; and this is something that must not be undervalued. It has become the fashion, with writers of the sentimental-international school, to decry national sentiment as a wholly mischievous and destructive thing, that stands in the way of the creation of a world-society, and must therefore—somehow—be conjured away by the persuasive arguments of these gentlemen. They need not imagine that an emotion so powerful will easily, or perhaps ever, be overcome by Niagaras of talk. To take such a view is to base their hopes and plans for a better world upon a false foundation. Nationalism is doubtless a dangerous factor, and may even be a destructive factor, in an interdependent world, especially when it is inflamed and excited, as it is to-day. But it is one of the supreme facts of which we have to take account, and we cannot brush it aside because it is inconvenient for our theories. The world of the future will, almost certainly, be a world of Nation-States. And it will be a world of Nation-States precisely because the national form of State can give, and has given, to its citizens certain benefits which no other form has yet been able to yield.

45

The first of these is that, because of the strength of the loyalty it has been able to evoke, it has succeeded in overcoming the lesser loyalties that stood in the way of human progress. The Nation-States succeeded, with a completeness never attained by the most powerful of military empires, in putting an end to local wars, and abolishing local tariffs and other obstacles to trade. No doubt the growing interdependence within the nation which resulted from growing trade provided a strong motive for the destruction of these obstacles. When one part of a country was producing wool and weaving it into cloth, another making cutlery, another pottery, when the farmers in one region were concentrating upon corn-production and those in another upon stock-breeding, and when all found their advantage in exchanging their surplus products for the products of other districts, this regional division of labour not only enriched the whole community, but inevitably and progressively destroyed the self-sufficiency that had once marked each little district; and local wars and local tariffs became more and more intolerable because they interfered with the normal life of the people, just as national wars and national tariffs now impede the well-being of the world. But these practical consequences of growing interdependence within a country were not of themselves powerful enough to put an end to the evils which had sprung from the tradition of local self-sufficiency and from local loyalties. They had to be reinforced by the larger loyalty of the nation. In Germany and in Italy, until they attained national unity, these local obstacles to national well-being were never overcome.

Only the strength of national sentiment could subdue the reluctance of the Yorkshireman to see his local products displaced by the products of Lancashire. When he had learnt to regard even the Lancashire-man as no longer a foreigner but an Englishman, somehow his trafficking came to seem no longer mischievous but advantageous. Is it conceivable that a larger loyalty than that of the nation will somehow come to the aid of common sense in teaching the nations that they will increase and not diminish their prosperity by encouraging the exchange of their various products? The prospects do not at the moment seem bright. But in any case it must be recognised that the Nation-State was able to make in this way a vitally important contribution to human progress, in the economic as well as in the political sphere.

A second virtue of the national State is that it is able to win from its citizens a more willing obedience to law, a more ready acceptance of new laws, and a readiness to co-operate in the enforcement of law, such as the non-national State seldom or never achieves. On the whole, the national States are the most law-abiding, because the laws and their agents are not regarded as the instruments of an external power, but as belonging to the nation; and patriot-ism reinforces authority in securing obedience to them. If America is an exception, it is the sort of exception that proves the rule : the lawlessness prevalent in the United States is in no small degree due to the variety of half-digested alien stocks that are included in the American society : the very names of Al Capone and other gangster leaders would

47

seem to bear out this view. When Italy was under Austrian control, and the ferment of nationalism was at work among the people, disobedience to the laws might well appear an evidence of patriotism; and in the India of to-day, where this ferment is actively at work, disobedience to laws which may be regarded (however incorrectly) as imposed by foreign rulers may also be exalted into a virtue. The character of law-abidingness, which is one of the most essential equipments of a civilised society, is certainly most easily cultivated in national States, wherein the nation's laws are part of that whole national ethos which patriotism upholds even in face of justified criticism.

A further virtue of the national State is that it makes self-government possible. It is only among a people united by common loyalties that government by discussion and agreement can work well; where there are sharp racial or religious cleavages, and fundamental disunities of outlook and purpose, willing submission to the decisions of a majority is not to be expected. For this reason, parliamentary government has never been successful except in Nation-States. In the Austro-Hungarian Empire before the war, with its numerous clashing peoples, Germans, Magyars, Czechs, Croats, Rumans, Slovenes, Serbs, the parliamentary system did not merely break down, it provided an arena in which the various races disputed with one another, and thereby exacerbated their differences, and prepared the way for the break-up of the Empire. Even in Britain, parliamentary government almost broke down when the Irish Nationalist party, concentrating all their attention upon a single object, refused to play the parliamentary game.

A type of State which secures ready obedience to the law, which inspires its subjects to make great sacrifices when sacrifices are needed for the service of the community, and which is the only kind of State wherein the most advanced and the most difficult form of government—government by discussion and agreement—can be efficiently carried on, assuredly renders immense services to humanity; and there is no reason for lamentation in the prospect of its becoming the normal type of State throughout the civilised world. But the insistence on " self-determination," the *sacro egoismo*, the pride that " fears God and nothing else on earth," the spirit of *sinn fein* (ourselves alone), which are characteristic of nationalism, while they may lead to no grave difficulties in an era when nations can be self-sufficient, offer very serious perils in an era of world-interdependence such as we have now entered; and before we pass to the consideration of the problems of, and the outlook for, this interdependent world, it is necessary to dwell for a little upon these dangerous aspects of nationalism.

IV. *The Dangers of Nationalism.*

The national spirit is proud, self-assertive, very sensitive of any slight to dignity or any diminution of prestige, and as ready to take offence as a fine gentleman in the age of duelling. That is why the language of diplomacy has to be so punctiliously courteous: plain speaking between nations is held to be out of the question, and the indiscretions of the popular press may be very dangerous. And, since submission to an outside judgment is still felt to be as wounding to the pride of a nation as the reference of an affair of honour to the law-courts would have seemed to any gentleman in the age of the duel, nationalism has always been prone to war. Nearly all the wars of Europe in the modern age can be traced to its influence. Some of them have been due to the masterful pride of strong and aggressive nations, such as the Spain of Philip II, the France of Louis XIV and Napoleon, the Germany of Wilhelm II; others to the aspirations of divided nations, such as the Italy and the Germany of 1850, to achieve unity, or of subject nations, such as the Balkan States, to win freedom. It cannot be easy for a world of nations so touchy and so bellicose to live in peace when their interests are so interlocked as they are in the modern world; they must find it difficult to accept their mutual dependence. Yet the establishment of a settled peace is essential not only to the progress, but to the very existence, of civilisation in modern conditions. Here lies the first great danger of nationalism. How is the prickly pride of the Nation-States to be accommodated with the needs of an interdependent world?

Nations have always regarded self-sufficiency as one of the essential attributes of nationhood. They aspire to be self-sufficient in regard to defence, to be able to defend their freedom, their interests and their honour, without dependence upon any power outside themselves. But in a world so closely interlocked as this world now is, no nation can be so strong as to be free from all danger, without also being so strong as to be a menace to its neighbours. In fact, self-sufficiency in defence is unattainable in an interdependent world; and the attempt to attain it may be ruinous.

Again, all nations have striven after economic self-sufficiency, and it is not very long since it was practically attainable. In the eighteenth century neither England nor France would have been ruined, though both would have been impoverished, if their trade with the rest of the world had been wholly cut off: they depended upon the rest of the world only for inessential luxuries. In the conditions of the modern world, as we have seen, economic self-sufficiency is utterly unattainable. But the more this state of things developed, the more the nations struggled to resist it. It is significant that the doctrine that economic self-sufficiency is a necessary attribute of nationhood obtained its clearest and most logical expression in Friedrich List's *National Economy*, just after Germany had achieved her unity—just when the national spirit in Europe was most significant; but at this very time the development of world-trade and the growing utilisation of tropical products were already making self-sufficiency unattainable for nations whose territory lay wholly in the temperate zone.

Two things followed. On the one hand came the eager rush of the European countries for extra-European and (in particular) tropical possessions, which led to the imperialist frenzy of the last quarter of the nineteenth century. On the other hand, the nations began building higher and higher tariff walls against one another, to save themselves from being reduced to dependence upon one another's products. The development of international commerce was retarded, and trade was distorted by nationalist sentiment. The trading activities of the various nations were regarded not as the means of co-operation for mutual enrichment, but as a form of war; and they certainly tended to provoke actual war. And when the Great War came to demonstrate that almost every form of industrial production was called into play for warlike purposes, and that no country could succeed in war unless it was highly developed in an industrial sense, and could produce its own scientific instruments, its own chemicals, its own metallurgical products, its own food-stuffs, the demand for economic self-sufficiency became fiercer than ever, and tariff walls were raised to higher and higher levels, until international trade was almost brought to a standstill, at the very moment when the economic interdependence of the world had become more obvious and more absolute than ever before. Thus the almost instinctive demand of nationalism for self-sufficiency, combined with the inherent bellicosity of the national spirit, constitutes a grave peril to an interdependent world.

Finally, all nations claim, as an essential element in their nationhood, the right of unlimited and inalienable sovereignty, which means that they must be the sole judges of their own rights and claims. The doctrine of State-sovereignty, which has long been treated as almost an axiom in the text-books of political science in every country, is, indeed, itself an outcome and expression of the national spirit.   The theory of State-sovereignty has only been developed during the period when the Nation-States dominated the political life of Europe; and it is only in our own days that its validity has begun to be challenged by a few political thinkers. But so long as it is almost everywhere treated as a self-evident proposition, so long any reasonable adjustment of the claims of nationalism to the needs and conditions of an interdependent world must be almost impossible.

Three conclusions seem to emerge from our survey of the working of the national spirit.   The first is that it has contributed very greatly to, and, indeed, has alone rendered possible, the remarkable expansion of European methods and ideas which has brought some sort of world-unity in sight.   The second is that it has provided an invaluable cement for large communities of mankind, and a sounder and more healthy foundation for the organisation of States than ever existed before.   The third is that its touchy pride, its desire for self-sufficiency, and its assertion of unqualified sovereignty make it a dangerous element in an interdependent world. The dangers which spring from this source have been very apparent since the war; we must consider them more fully in the next chapter.

CHAPTER III

An interdependent world, such as we described in the first chapter, which consists of independent nations claiming unlimited sovereignty and striving after self-sufficiency, such as we described in the second chapter, must be a very insecure and precarious world, unless and until the component nations have learnt to recognise and accept their interdependence, to base their whole policy upon it, and to establish in co-operation the institutions necessary to make interdependence tolerable. For each nation, or at any rate each of the more powerful nations, has it in its power to make the system of interdependence not merely unworkable, but a source of disaster to itself and to all the rest, if it insists upon pursuing to their logical conclusion the desire for self-sufficiency and the claim to unlimited sovereignty.

In the present chapter we propose to analyse the inherent dangers of this situation in the two spheres of politics and economics. In both spheres, the course of events since the war has very powerfully illustrated the nature of these dangers. All the miseries of the world during the last few years are directly traceable to the failure of the world to recognise the fact of its interdependence, and the

54

perils that inhere in this state of things. And although it is impossible to separate rigidly the political from the economic sphere, it will be convenient, at the risk of some overlapping, to deal with them in turn.

I. *The Political Perils of Interdependence.*

(a) *The Peril of War.*

In the relations between States, the *ultima ratio*, throughout the course of human history, has always been war; and the idea of the inevitability of war is so deeply rooted in the traditions of all peoples that it is very difficult to eradicate. Even when States have settled their differences without resort to war—as when the imperialist peoples of Europe partitioned Africa by a series of peaceful agreements —the possibility of war, and calculations of the power of different States if war should come, were always the ruling factors in the background, determining the settlement. And this must always be the case, so long as there does not exist some alternative method of settling differences to which every nation will be compelled to resort by the strength of the whole society of nations.

The use of war as the ultimate determinant did not seem, to earlier generations of men, the moral enormity which it has rapidly come to appear in the eyes of this generation, and that for several reasons. Few of the wars of the modern era, waged as they mostly were by small professional armies and between economically self-sufficient countries, very seriously dislocated the life of the peoples who were engaged in them. The peoples might be impoverished by heavier taxes than usual, and disturbed by billetings and forced recruitment; but for the most part their life went on in its normal way. No war of modern times (before the Great War) has in fact ever threatened the absolute and irretrievable ruin of any people. Moreover, very few (if any) wars have been utterly unjustifiable, seeing that the mind of man is so constituted that (except when he has adopted fighting as a profession) he will not fight with enthusiasm unless he can be persuaded that there is justice on his side—a fact of which even despotic governments have had to take some account. In short, until recently, war did not appear to be a crime against civilisation, since it often led to progress, and was often the means of rectifying injustice; moreover, it was often demonstrably advantageous to the victor, and sometimes to his conquered subjects.

In the conditions of the world of to-day, and with the methods of warfare which have been brought into existence by improved communications and by the hideous powers of destruction that have been made available by science, war, on any scale larger than mere police operations, has become a crime against civilisation.

In an interdependent world, every part of which relies for its livelihood upon resources drawn from every other part, a great war dislocates completely the normal life of men. It calls into the battle-line no longer merely a few professional soldiers, but the whole manhood of all the peoples engaged, and indirectly the whole population. It severs without mercy the myriad interlacing filaments of trade by which the modern world is kept alive. It employs weapons of destruction which are not only barbarous but indiscriminate in their operation. It can wipe out whole cities, destroy the nerve-centres of national life, and bring whole societies to a ruin more complete than was ever possible in any earlier age.

Moreover, war can no longer bring any advantage even to the victor. When, some years before the Great War, a distinguished writer, Sir Norman Angell, pointed out that the conditions of modern life made war not merely ruinous but utterly futile, he was jeered at by many critics. Events have proved the truth of his thesis. We have seen the victors in a great war brought to the verge of bankruptcy, striving to alleviate their distress by exacting huge penalties from the vanquished, and discovering that the attempt to obtain relief in this way was foredoomed to failure, and only added to their own distresses by disorganising the trade of the interdependent world. Having become not only ruinous but futile, war can no longer be, in an interdependent world, the *ultima ratio* in the relations between nations, except at the cost of whelming them all in a common destruction.

The change in the aspect of world-politics which has been brought about by the coming of interdependence, and by the development of scientific methods of destruction, is best illustrated by the changed position of Britain, which is in many ways the most representative country of the modern world. What is true of Britain is true of other countries also in a less degree; but it is more obviously and more sensationally true of Britain than of any other country.

For nine centuries Britain has been the safest country in the world in which to dwell. Since the Norman Conquest no invading army has ever succeeded in establishing itself on her shores, unless it came by invitation; and no other country has such a record of security. She has owed this security to her insular position, and to her navy: no other country has ever had such good reason for trusting to armaments for its safety. The character of her people, the nature of her institutions, the development of her trade, the creation of her world-wide empire, in short all the most distinctive features of her history, have been due to this unique security. And now, in the conditions of the modern world, this age-long security has gone for ever, and can never be regained by anything that Britain herself can do: it can only be restored under the protection of a collective system of peace, guaranteeing security equally to all nations.

This revolution (for it is no less) in the position of Britain has been brought about by two factors— by the effects of interdependence, and by the methods of modern warfare. There is no country which is more utterly dependent for her existence upon the rest of the world: most of the food her people eat, and most of the raw materials of her industry, must come from overseas, and must be paid for by the products of her factories, sent overseas. Her life therefore depends upon the inward and outward cargoes of her ships; and if these should be interrupted, half of her population must die of starvation.

The Great War showed that these supplies *can* be interrupted. Half-a-dozen German surface-raiders were able to do infinite damage in distant seas, and according to Lord Jellicoe it took 140 cruisers to hunt them down. If the enemy had not possessed a very short coast-line, easily blockaded, or if Britain had not been helped by all but one of the great navies of the world, there would have been many more raiders, and the results might have been fatal. To provide against this peril, not 140 but 1400 cruisers would be necessary. Again, the submarine, which was only in its infancy in the Great War, nearly brought Britain to starvation in 1917, though Germany had only a small number of these vessels, and did not use them ruthlessly until two years had been spent in the laying of nets and mines and other safeguards against them. What would happen if a large number of submarines were suddenly launched from a country with a long coast-line and many lurking-places, and with no time given for the provision of safeguards?

Finally, the development of aerial warfare, which, like the submarine, was in its infancy during the war, has deprived Britain of her insular security. For the first time in English history British subjects were in the last war killed by enemy action in the very streets of London. Armed with bombs filled with poison-gas, modern aircraft can depopulate a city in a night or two, and no country offers to attack such congested masses of population as Britain. Against this attack there is no defence:

neither armies nor ships nor aircraft themselves are of any avail against a sudden onslaught; and there is no kind of warfare in which the victim can be more completely taken by surprise. In these conditions, Britain has become, instead of the safest, the most unsafe country in the world in time of war: her insular position has become a danger instead of an advantage: the island that was a fortress has become a trap.

In another war of the same scale as the last, Britain would run the risk of being starved into surrender, and also of seeing London and other cities, which are the nerve-centres of her life, obliterated. She would be faced by a ruin more terrible and more complete than has ever in history faced any great State. The same possibilities of utter ruin overhang, though less terribly, every other State in the world; and as the dizzy progress of science goes on with accelerating rapidity, so does man's capacity for destroying the civilisation he has built up. The power of setting at work these horrific means of destruction lies in the hands of every State, so long as all continue to wield irresponsible sovereignty. This interdependent world of sovereign States is like a schoolroom full of children, each brandishing a stick of dynamite.

There is only one safeguard against this peril— only one possible means of restoring to Britain the security to which she has become accustomed, and which has fixed the character of her national life, and of giving to other nations a security such as most of them have never known. It is that, by the will of all the nations, war should cease to be the *ultima ratio* which it has always hitherto been in the relations between States, and should be banished from the earth as a crime against civilisation; and this can only be done by the establishment of a collective system whereby not only security but justice shall be guaranteed to all peoples. This (as we shall see in the next chapter) involves nothing less than a revolution in the traditional ideas of all peoples. It involves a definite limitation by the common will of that irresponsible sovereignty which nations have always regarded as essential to their national freedom.

Here, then, is the first of the dangers of inter-dependence in a world of sovereign nations—the danger that civilisation may be blotted out, or at any rate that the very existence of some of the nations may be destroyed, by the irresponsible action of any member of the interdependent world.

(b) *The Extension of Self-Determination.*

Among the European peoples, the idea of national freedom has always been identified with the ideas of national self-sufficiency, and of unlimited national sovereignty. It is this identification which has made nationalism so great a danger in an interdependent world. But the desire for national freedom, and for organisation in the national form of State, is spreading rapidly over the globe. If these other ideas, which have done so much harm in Europe, are extended to the rest of the world, there will lie before us a limitless vista of conflict and impover-ishment, which will for generations prevent the human race from enjoying the well-being that is within its grasp.

The identification of national freedom with self-sufficiency and irresponsible sovereignty is not necessary. We have recently seen in Europe outstanding examples in which a reasonable degree of foresight could have prevented it, and in which failure to exercise this foresight has done infinite harm.

The erection of the so-called Succession States on the ruins of the Austro-Hungarian Empire is one such example. Beyond doubt it was to the advantage of these peoples, and to the advantage of the world, that they should have the fullest freedom to develop their own civilisation in their own way, for long experience had shown that they could not be happy in forced union. Yet their establishment as sovereign States has brought two great evils: it has impoverished these States themselves, and Europe as a whole, through the erection across old and well-defined trade-routes of new tariff-walls, five of which now exist where only one existed before the war; and it has gravely added to the danger of war by setting up five States all armed to the teeth, and all regarding one another with jealousy and fear. These were not necessary consequences of national freedom; and there were two stages at which these evils could have been averted by statesmanlike foresight.

If, in 1850 or in 1867, the rulers of the Austro-Hungarian Empire had been willing (and the idea was at both dates suggested to them) to turn their empire into a federation of small nations, linked together by a customs union and by a common system of defence, not only would the Austro-Hungarian Empire have survived and played a valuable part in the life of Europe, but the small States on its fringes which had racial affinities with various members of the federation—notably Rumania and Serbia—might have become members of the federation, and in course of time Bulgaria, Albania, and perhaps Greece, might have come in. This would have been the ideal solution for the troubles of south-eastern Europe. It would have reconciled national freedom in all essentials with the avoidance of economic and military rivalry; and it would almost certainly have averted the Great War. The failure of statesmanship to seize this opportunity sentenced the Austro-Hungarian Empire to disruption, and its parts to conflict and impoverishment.

Another opportunity came in 1919, when these peoples received the gift of freedom from the victorious allies. It might even then have been possible (though it would have been more difficult) to link these peoples in a federal union. It would certainly have been possible to impose upon them, as a condition of their freedom, a limitation of armaments and a limitation of tariffs, perhaps within an expansible customs union. This opportunity also was lost, because the superstition of " self-determination " held the field—as if any nation *could* determine its own destiny without regard to its neighbours in an interdependent world!—and this superstition was held to involve the enjoyment by every nation of unlimited sovereignty, economic and political.

Another illustration of the same lack of foresight has been provided by the case of Ireland. If the ruling classes in Britain, fifty years ago, had had sufficient imagination to see that the nationalist spirit in Ireland was too powerful to be disregarded or overridden, they could have ensured—indeed, under the Home Rule Bills of 1886 and 1892 they *would* have ensured—that Ireland should enjoy all the essentials of national freedom, and every opportunity to deal with her own problems in her own way, without the necessity for that miserable economic war with her greater neighbour into which she has recently been drawn by inherited distrust and fantastically exaggerated nationalism, and which can do nothing but harm to both parties, and consequently to the world.

The British Empire as a whole affords, on a vast scale, yet another example of the same failure to recognise that the sound principle of national freedom may easily be carried to a dangerous extreme. When the Liberals of the nineteenth century, inspired by the fine and generous idea that the colonies should be encouraged to develop their own modes of life in the fullest freedom, granted the complete rights of self-government to each of them in turn, it ought to have been possible to provide that there should be no tariff barriers within the Empire, whatever restrictions upon external trade its members might choose to impose; and that there should be a single common system of defence. The latter aim was in effect secured (in an unsatisfactory way), because both Britain and the colonies were content that Britain should con-

tinue to bear practically the whole cost of imperial
defence, except in India. The Lord Grey of that
date made some attempt, in the 'fifties, to secure a
common economic system. But it was then, perhaps, already too late. It was assumed as an axiom
that the pursuit of self-sufficiency was an essential
element in national freedom; with the result that
to-day we see the members of this fellowship of
peoples engaged in sordid bargainings which cannot
but strain their friendship, and which must increase
the difficulty of any wider movement towards world-
fellowship.

The difficulty, in any case stupendously great, of
working out a system of self-government suitable for
the 320,000,000 people of infinitely varied races,
languages, religions, and stages of civilisation, who
constitute the Indian Empire, has been immensely
accentuated by the interpretation which Indians
have been encouraged to put upon the mischievous
phrase " self-determination " by the example of the
European peoples whose institutions and methods
they are eager to imitate. India has given much,
and has much more to give, to the rest of the world;
she has drawn much from the rest of the world,
and needs to draw much more; but if the acquisition
of political liberty is to mean that she will aim at
self-sufficiency and strive to withdraw herself from
contact with the rest of the world, and that she is
to claim complete and unlimited sovereignty, a free
India, instead of being a powerful contributor to
the well-being of the world, will be an obstacle to
it. And if this conception of what national freedom means is to be adopted also in China, and in

F   65

all the other lands to which this aspiration is spreading, the outlook for the future is grim indeed.

It is from Europe that the ideal of national liberty has spread over the globe—a great gift, and potentially a great contribution to the world's well-being. But with this gift of the idea of liberty have been associated two other ideas which are noxious, the ideas of self-sufficiency and of unlimited sovereignty as necessary conditions of national freedom. The influence of Europe in the non-European world is dwindling, precisely because, hag-ridden by these two ideas, Europe is finding herself unable to solve her own problems. She will only solve these problems, and she will only regain the leadership of the world, if she discards the false ideas that are ruining herself and the world. If she can do so, she will immensely contribute to ease the difficulties that arise from the extension of the spirit of nationalism over the globe.

II. *The Economic Perils of Interdependence.*

The troubled years since the war have provided the world with a demonstration of the dangers that attend interdependence in the economic as well as in the political sphere, so long as no appropriate system of common regulation exists. It is not only that the self-regarding policies of the nations have stood in the way of the world's enjoyment of the prosperity that is within its reach: this prosperity cannot be fully enjoyed unless, in certain spheres, the nations do not merely abstain from impeding it, but actively co-operate to bring it about.

The state of the world since the war presents,

indeed, an astonishing paradox. The world is producing, or can produce, all the goods that are
requisite for the material well-being of mankind in
greater abundance and variety, with a vastly smaller
outlay of labour, and therefore at a much lower
cost, than ever before; moreover, its productive
capacity grows year by year. The methods of
transport have been so marvellously perfected that
the products of every part of the world can rapidly
and cheaply be made available for every other part.
In these conditions there seems to be no reason why
the whole human race should not now be enjoying a
universally diffused well-being, such as has never
hitherto been within its reach. Yet at this moment
all the peoples of the earth are submerged in a
common distress. The producers of commodities
which are in universal demand cannot get a price for
them that covers the cost of production, and therefore
cannot buy the goods they themselves want: barns
and warehouses are filled with unsaleable surpluses,
and supplies of corn, of coffee, of rubber, which the
world could well use, are being burnt for fuel. Some
25,000,000 workers are without work or wages, in
all the industrial countries, and the purchasing
power which they might be using is unavailable.
The producers of food-stuffs want boots and clothes,
and can't buy them; the producers of boots and
clothes want more food-stuffs, and can't buy them.
How has this vicious circle come into being? What
is wrong with the world's machinery of trade that is
making it impossible for the world's abundance to
go where it is needed in return for the labour of
those who produce it?

Three things would seem to be necessary if all the peoples of the earth are to enjoy the plenty which the earth produces. The first is that there should be the greatest possible freedom of exchange for the products of all countries, without needless impediments or artificial increases in price. The second is that there should be in each country a sufficiency of money, corresponding with the value of the country's products, to serve as the medium of exchange at home and abroad; and that the moneys of various countries should exchange one against the other at a steady level. The third is that the money which represents the value of production should be wisely distributed between spending and saving, and that spending power should be fairly shared by all who contribute to the work of production, in proportion to the value of their contributions. Not one of these three conditions is adequately met in the world as it now is; and that is (broadly) why the world is starving in the midst of plenty. None of these conditions can be satisfactorily met except by international co-operation, though individual countries can follow a wiser or a more foolish policy in regard to each of them. Thus an individual country can give to its citizens unimpeded access to the wealth of the world, as Britain did until recently; but this policy cannot have its full effect unless all other countries pursue it. Thus, again, an individual country can establish a sound monetary system; but international trade will only thrive if all the principal countries adopt monetary systems planned on the same sound lines. Thus, finally, an individual country can pursue an enlightened policy in the distribution of wealth; but it cannot go far on this path unless other countries are prepared to walk in. step with it.

What has gone wrong with the world's economic system in recent years is that there has been a lack of the needful co-operation in each of these spheres —far less than there was before the war, at any rate in respect of freedom of interchange, and money; because all the nations have been pursuing their individual advantage, imagining that they could attain it at the expense of their neighbours, and failing to see that, in an interdependent world, a narrowly conceived national policy brings its own punishment more surely than in a world which has not yet become interdependent. Let us consider in turn how and why the world has suffered from the disregard of interdependence in each of these spheres—freedom of international exchange, sound money, and just distribution.

(a) *The Peril of Tariff Restrictions.*

Before the Great War, almost the whole world had adopted the protectionist system of restricting trade in order to give the home producer an advantage over the foreign producer. Alone among the great industrial and trading countries, Britain remained loyal to the system of free imports which she had adopted seventy years before, and under which all foreign products were admitted to her markets on the same terms as her home products.

This policy had not ruined her; on the contrary, on the eve of the war she had reached the highest point of prosperity which she had ever attained in her history. Her industries were thriving. She enjoyed, in proportion to her population, a vastly larger share of the world's trade than any other country. She owned half of the world's shipping, built more new ships every year than all other countries put together, and did an enormous proportion of the world's carrying trade. She owed her supremacy in this field to her fiscal policy, which gave her access to the materials for shipbuilding at the lowest world-prices, while the constant coming and going of goods to and from her open ports provided cargoes for her ships. She had become the world's central market, because buyers from every other country knew that they could obtain in Britain supplies of all the world's products at the lowest prices, unimpeded by duties; and this had enabled her to build up an immense entrepôt or re-export trade. For the same reason, she had become the pivot of the world's financial system: most of the world's trade was carried on by means of bills on London, which were acceptable everywhere because there was no part of the world that did not trade with Britain; and in effect the London money-market managed the world's money-system, which worked pretty smoothly. She had been for two generations the main purveyor of capital for the development of the world's resources; which meant that she had provided from her factories the material necessary for the equipment of other countries (especially new countries) with railways, factories, harbours, etc., receiving payment in annual interest, which came in the form of vast supplies of the goods of the debtor countries. Some of these goods her own people consumed, some were used as the materials of her own industries, to be sold at home or abroad, some were re-exported to other countries in the forms in which they came. If she had adopted a tariff policy, the payment of the interest on her foreign investments would have been seriously impeded.

The proof of the success of her policy was visible in the fact that she was able to provide for her crowded population a far higher standard of living, as measured by wage-rates, than any but the new countries with their unexhausted resources were able to achieve, and she maintained a more generous system of social services for the relief of distress and the improvement of the physical and mental condition of her people than any other country. During the period of her loyalty to free trade, the average wage-levels of her workers had actually been multiplied fourfold, money wages being doubled while the purchasing power of the pound was also doubled. If the object of a nation's economic policy is to bring about a steady and continuous improvement in the standard of living of its people—and no better object can be defined—then, assuredly, the economic policy of Britain had been fully justified by success. She had obtained these results in spite of the fact that her natural resources were far inferior to those of her principal rivals, America and Germany; and in spite of the further fact that she had allowed herself to fall seriously behind these rivals in the utilisation of science and research. The final test of the success of her policy was afforded by the war. Alone among the European allies, all of whom save herself were protectionist, she was able by her own resources to stand the colossal strain of war; nay, she was able, until the last stages of the war, to finance not only her own activities, but in a large degree those of her allies. And when the war was over, despite the fact that she had been compelled to sacrifice, while war lasted, the bulk of her foreign trade, her credit still stood higher than that of any of the European belligerents, and she alone avoided the financial collapse which all of them had to face in the years immediately following the war.

Britain, it might seem, had given an object-lesson to the rest of the world as to the kind of trade-policy suitable to modern conditions. The first of all countries to be forced to realise her dependence upon the rest of the world, she had based her whole policy upon the recognition and acceptance of inter-dependence, and had given to her people unimpeded access to all that the world produced. The other nations had been slow to follow her lead, just as, in another sphere, they had been slow to imitate her great experiment of representative government. They were all still striving after the end of self-sufficiency, which was becoming more and more unattainable. They were all still convinced that they could all enrich themselves at one another's expense, and that international trade was a form of rivalry or war, not a mutual interchange of benefits. Moreover, in all protectionist countries—it is one of the inevitable consequences of the system—powerful vested interests had grown up, among producers who profited (or believed that they profited) by being enabled to charge higher prices to their home purchasers more than they lost by being compelled to pay higher prices for their own requirements; and as these vested interests were small in numbers, concentrated, and influential, they could always get the better of the diffused and unorganised interests of the consumers.

It is not surprising, therefore, that the other nations had not followed Britain along the path of free trade. If they had all done so during the half-century before the war, the whole aspect of the world would have changed. Innumerable causes of friction would have disappeared; the fierce conflict for reserved and exclusive markets, which was one of the chief causes of the imperialist rivalry that preceded and helped to cause the war, would have been appeased; and the war would probably never have taken place. Britain might have lost the pre-eminence in shipping, in entrepôt trade, in financial business, and in foreign investment, which she owed to the fact that she was the only great free-trade country; but this would have been far more than balanced by an immense increase in world-trade in which she would have had her share, though she might have been handicapped by her tardiness in adopting modern and scientific methods of production.

Unquestionably Britain was hurt by the tariffs which almost all other countries maintained; but she was not so much hurt by them as the tariff countries themselves. Moreover, in the years before the war the obstacles to the growth of world-trade were materially lessened by two facts. In the first place, there were innumerable commercial treaties which qualified the severity of tariffs; and Britain, because she gave an open market to all countries, enjoyed the advantages of " the most favoured nation" under all these treaties. In the second place, while a new and increased tariff may inflict sudden damage upon many industries, as time passes this evil rectifies itself in some degree; for the tariff does not only hit the foreign trader, it increases all the costs of the domestic producer; and when this effect is fully felt, it often becomes once more possible for the foreign trader, owing to his lower costs, to overleap the tariff. That is why, once a country is committed to the protectionist system, it finds itself driven by the clamours of its own producers, and by the logic of its own theory, to frequent upward revisions. In the years before the war, however, tariffs were more or less stable. They therefore constituted less of an obstacle to international trade than might have been anticipated; the volume of international trade went on increasing, and Britain, overleaping many of the tariffs because of her low costs, got her full share of the increase.

When the war came to an end, and the nations recognised their interdependence, at all events in the political sphere, by establishing the League of Nations, it might have been expected that they would recognise it also in the economic sphere by adopting the policy of free trade. They never thought of doing so. Nationalist feeling had been aroused to a high pitch by the war, and economic self-sufficiency was universally regarded as an essential attribute of national freedom. One of the first acts of the new States was to build tariff walls against their neighbours; and these new tariff walls were not modified, like their predecessors, by a system of commercial treaties, because most of the commercial treaties had been terminated by the war.

Moreover, the war itself seemed to have provided a new argument for economic self-sufficiency. It was evident that no country was safe in war unless it could feed itself, and that modern warfare could not be efficiently carried on by any country that did not possess highly developed industries, notably the metallurgical and the chemical industries. All countries therefore set themselves to foster these industries by means of tariffs, in order to be ready for war. Even Britain departed to some extent from her free-trade system by passing an Act for the Safeguarding of Key Industries—the Key Industries being those that were most necessary for war—and also an Act for the protection of the dye-stuffs industry, because it was closely connected with the chemical trades that produced poison gas. The fear of war was still predominant, League or no League; and the fear of war dictated a policy of self-sufficiency.

Other considerations told in the same direction. When the currencies of many countries collapsed, it was feared that the countries thus affected would have a great advantage in export trade, because the decline in the value of their money reduced the burden of their fixed charges, and also reduced the cost of wages, which always lag behind rising prices. These fears were not fully justified, but they provided the excuse for still further tariff increases, which were directed not only against the countries with depreciating currencies, but against all countries; and when currencies were stabilised, these duties were not withdrawn, because powerful vested interests had been created. Again, the forced payment of German reparations and later of war-debts involved a large outpouring of exports from the debtor countries without any commercial return. The very countries which insisted that Germany must pay raised their tariffs in order to prevent her from paying in the only possible way, by exporting her goods.

Thus everything contributed to bring about in the post-war world a mania of tariffs, which bade fair to bring international trade to a standstill, prevented the world from enjoying the abundance which it was producing, and in some commodities caused over-production, by forcing on the production of these commodities in countries which were not specially adapted to produce them.

The mounting tariffs of the post-war years were so visibly strangling the trade of the world that in 1927, at an economic conference held at Geneva and attended by official representatives of fifty nations, the subject was brought up for discussion. All the delegates—many of whom were officials responsible for the drafting of tariff schedules—unanimously agreed that very great harm was being done; that tariffs (though within the " sovereignty " of each nation) were a matter of international concern; and that it was essential to the well-being of the world that the upward movement, which had been so marked since the war, should be reversed. But this conclusion had no direct results; it was not even

found possible to negotiate a " tariff truce "—
indeed, the Conservative party in Britain strongly
objected to this proposal, being bent upon committing
their own country to a systematic tariff policy. The
nations could not be persuaded that it was impossible
for them to enrich themselves by restricting their
trade.

Then came the world-wide economic and financial
crisis of 1929 and the following years. It was
largely the outcome of the follies of the previous
period, among which the rivalry of tariffs took
the first place; for even the monetary difficulties
of the time, and the concentration of the world's
gold supply in France and America, were due to the
working of the tariff system. As the crisis deepened,
panic took possession of the governments; and the
only remedies they could think of for a state of things
that was mainly due to the restriction of trade was
to invent more restrictions for trade—higher tariffs,
prohibitions, import quotas, restrictions on the
transfer of currency—all of which had, and could
have, only one effect: to make the crisis more acute.

Instead of realising that there was no possibility of
prosperity for any country except through the
economic well-being of the interdependent world
as a whole, every nation strove to save itself at the
expense of its neighbours. It was a case of *sauve
qui peut*: each of the roped climbers desperately
strove to pull down or to kick down his neighbours,
or to hide himself in a funk-hole of his own, instead
of all co-operating to get out of the crevasse. They
trusted to tariff-walls to keep out the rising tide of
depression, but these impediments only made the

swirling stream fiercer. Was unemployment high? Tariffs were to cure it, by keeping out " dumped foreign goods "; but they also kept *in* the home products which would have gone to pay for these goods, and put out of work those who would have made them; while, by raising the cost of living, they reduced the purchasing power of the home market. Was revenue shrinking and expenditure rising, so that the Budget was unbalanced? Tariffs were to cure that also, by raising great revenues. But there is no source of revenue more expensive than a protective tariff, because, by raising the price of home products as well as foreign products, it takes out of the pocket of the consumer far more than the government receives, while it also hampers all the export trades by increasing their costs of production, and in this way sacrifices a great deal more than it gains. Were prices sinking to an intolerably low level, so that the producers were unable to buy their normal requirements? Tariffs were to cure that also, by raising prices. But in doing so, they made it more difficult for the producers in other countries to sell their goods, and therefore forced them to accept still more ruinous prices: to raise prices artificially within an individual country offered no remedy at all for the low level of world-prices, but accentuated it. A localised rise of prices which is due to a restriction of supply is a very different thing from a general rise of prices which is due to an increase of demand; and while tariffs might bring about the first, they could only impede the second. Was money unduly scarce, owing to the concentration of gold in two countries, caused by tariffs?

Restrictions upon the export of currency was the chosen remedy in many countries; but this only meant that, in the absence of the recognised medium of exchange, international trade was brought to a standstill, except through the cumbrous processes of barter. Was a country threatened by the awful nightmare of an " adverse trade balance," that is to say, was it in danger of buying more than it sold, or getting more than it gave, in the interchange of international trade? For this also tariffs were the accepted remedy, because they would reduce imports, and therefore perhaps prevent them from outweighing exports. But reflection ought to have shown, what experience quickly demonstrated, that it is impossible to cut down imports without also cutting down the exports that pay for them. The superstitious fear of an " adverse balance of trade," and the superstitious value attached to a " favourable balance of trade," were indeed among the most powerful influences which brought to its height the economic insanity of these years. Blind to the fact that it was in the nature of things impossible for *all* countries to sell more than they bought, they all set to work to restrict their imports, only to find that, as everybody else was doing the same thing, their exports were reduced in proportion; by the combined efforts of all the nations, it seemed likely that the currents of world-trade would be brought to a total stoppage.

So long as Britain remained a free-trade country, there was one important safety-valve, and the pressure upon it became very severe. But in 1931 Britain also fell a prey to the mania of economic

79

nationalism, persuading herself that by means of tariffs she could keep depression at bay, cure unemployment, raise revenue to balance the budget, raise prices, keep her currency steady, and secure a favourable balance of trade—the same illusions that had misled the other nations. The last safety-valve had been closed.

Such were the consequences of the unanimous attempt of the nations to achieve self-sufficiency, and to enrich themselves at one another's expense, in an interdependent world. All of them together were brought to the verge of ruin; and their only chance of an escape from disaster was to be found in collective action. All this tariff frenzy might have done comparatively little harm a hundred years ago, when nearly all countries really were almost self-sufficient. It was ruinous in the post-war period, precisely because, as we saw in the first chapter, interdependence had become the dominant and ineluctable fact in the life of the world.

(b) *The Peril of Monetary Collapse.*

The second peril in the economic sphere which interdependence has brought to the world is the peril of a monetary breakdown.

Before the nineteenth century, when each country could be almost self-sufficient, and international commerce was limited to inessential luxuries, it did not very seriously matter that the moneys of various countries should fluctuate in relation one to another, because the small volume of the traffic between them could be carried on by barter, or by the use of the precious metals, which had their value in all countries. But in an interdependent world, in which all peoples depend for many of their requirements upon supplies drawn from other countries, there are so many money transactions between one country and another that it becomes extremely important that the moneys of all the principal countries should maintain a steady value in relation to each other. Hence the question of money has ceased to be solely the concern of each country for itself, and has become an international problem, affecting deeply the welfare of the whole interdependent world-society, and only capable of being satisfactorily managed in co-operation.

It has always been one of the most important functions of government in every country to try to secure that the money which the government authorises shall have a steady value, that is to say, shall always be exchangeable for approximately the same amount of " things-in-general." For money depends for its validity upon governments, since it consists of certificates, or tickets-for-goods, guaranteed by a government and made legal tender within its jurisdiction, authorising the holder to obtain goods up to the value shown by it; and if the value or purchasing-power of these certificates is subject to sudden fluctuations, people will find that what they get in return for the goods or services they supply is sometimes greater and sometimes less, and the whole economic process is apt to be disorganised.

To keep the value of a country's money steady in relation to " things-in-general " is no easy matter. It is not less difficult to secure that the moneys of different countries shall be stable in relation to one another; and indeed this might seem to be impossible unless the chief countries can agree upon a common policy. Yet it is of vital importance that there should be stability both in the value of the money of each country within itself, and in the relative value of the money of different countries, otherwise the incessant exchange of goods and services which " makes the world go round " must be very seriously impaired.

Before the war, all the principal countries, without any formal agreement, had reached a common system, which—in spite of the absence of any central system of regulation—worked surprisingly well. Beginning with Britain, then the pivot of the world's economic system, whose example was followed by all the rest, they had adopted what is known as the Gold Standard; that is to say, they had decided that their money should always be equivalent in value to a fixed amount of gold—so much for the pound, so much for the dollar, so much for the mark; and to ensure that this should always be so, they had by law required their Central Banks always to buy and sell gold on demand, in exchange for a fixed amount of their money. It followed that the amount of money which any country could issue was necessarily limited by the amount of gold which its Central Bank had in stock: it must have enough to meet all probable demands, otherwise the system would break down.

This system had certain obvious advantages, and certain obvious dangers. It had the great advantage that the value of the money of each country was automatically fixed in relation to gold, and could not be tampered with by the government. But this was attended by the corresponding disadvantage that if gold (which varies in price, like any other commodity, according as it is scarce or plentiful) became too scarce and dear, the prices of goods (measured in gold) would go down, and all creditors would be enriched and all debtors impoverished. The danger was a real one, especially in a period of rapidly expanding trade, because the more goods have to be bought and sold, the more money will be needed with which to buy and sell them; and if gold is too scarce, too little money will be issued. But this danger did not materialise during the nineteenth century, because the new gold-finds in California, Australia, South Africa and the Klondyke roughly kept pace with the expanding needs of trade. To-day the output of gold is tending to decrease, and no big new gold-finds are likely; and this may constitute a difficulty in the future.

The second great advantage of the Gold Standard was that, as all the chief trading nations had adopted it, all their moneys kept, within very narrow limits, a fixed value in exchange for one another; and this immensely facilitated international trade, and largely accounted for its rapid growth during the later nineteenth century. But this advantage also had a corresponding danger. The Gold Standard could only work on an international basis if the world's stock of gold was fairly distributed among the various countries in proportion to their needs. If any country accumulated gold on a great scale, and thereby left the rest with too little of it, the result would be to disorganise the system. How could this danger be avoided without some kind of inter-national regulation? It was done, in fact, down to the war, by means of the financial leadership wielded by the City of London, whose bankers and financiers understood monetary questions better than those of any other country. Britain being then the central market and the great creditor-country of the world, gold poured into London; but it was never allowed to accumulate; it was kept moving in the settlement of international balances and the issue of loans; and so the Gold Standard worked well.

The coming of war at once broke down the Gold Standard. All countries needed so much money to pay the cost of wholesale destruction that it was impossible to limit the output of money according to Gold Standard rules. There was no longer any automatic limit upon the printing of money by governments: there was wholesale " inflation "—that is to say, an increase of money without any corresponding increase of wealth; and consequently prices rose steeply, because, since money was relatively more plentiful than goods, more money had to be given for a given amount of goods.

After the war, nearly all the governments of Europe allowed this process to continue, and lost control of it. They all spent more than they raised by taxation, and met the balance by printing money. The more money they printed, the more they had to print, and the more people lost confidence in their money; some of the currencies of Europe so completely lost their value that the nominal equivalent of (say) £10,000 had to be paid for a loaf of bread. In these circumstances all claims that

were defined in terms of money, such as holdings of
national debt or savings bank deposits, lost their
value, and all debts were practically wiped out.
The German who had invested (say) 20,000 marks
(nominally £1,000) in war loan found that his
marks, which used to buy as much as English shillings,
were worth less than a millionth part of a penny : his
savings had vanished into thin air. This chaos,
besides causing an immense amount of suffering and
loss, was ruinous to trade ; because no trader knew
what would be the value to-morrow of the money he
received to-day. Europe obtained such a lesson on
the evils of inflation as she would not soon forget.
But the real cause of inflation, and of all the sufferings
it brought, was the fact that the world's monetary
system, which had worked well enough before the
war, had broken down ; and that there was no
common authority able to restore it—every country
was going its own way.

Meanwhile America and Britain had followed a
different course. America had accumulated a huge
stock of gold during the war, far more than she needed
for monetary purposes ; and it was therefore easy for
her to maintain the Gold Standard and to guarantee
that every dollar should be worth the same amount
of gold as before the war. It was not so easy for
Britain, because she had been compelled by war
needs to issue very large amounts of money, so much
that it was quite impossible for her to guarantee the
pre-war gold value of the pound. In 1921 and the
following years, she set herself to restore the old
value of the pound by " deflation," that is, by
reducing the amount of her money in circulation,

until in 1925 she was able to announce that she had returned to the Gold Standard, and that in future the Bank of England would buy or sell gold on demand at the old fixed rate in British money.

But, of course, the effect of reducing the amount of money in circulation was to bring about a steady fall of prices in Britain; because, when money was scarce, more goods had to be given in exchange for it, or, to put it the other way round, the producer of goods got less money for his products. On the other hand, the owner of national debt or other fixed-interest securities, though he got the same number of pounds, was able to buy many more goods with them, while the real value of all wages fixed in money was similarly increased. The result was that the burden of debts and taxes and the real cost of wages (measured in the goods that had to be produced to pay for them) were enormously increased; industry was crippled by these burdens; Britain lost more and more of her export trade in competition with countries which were not similarly burdened; and the figures for unemployment increased in an alarming way.

Evidently " deflation " was as bad in its way as " inflation." What the world needed was a stable value of money, and a steady level of prices; and the cause of all these sufferings was, that instead of co-operating to restore a sound monetary system for a disorganised but still interdependent world, all the nations had gone on their own way, independently, believing that independent control of their monetary systems was an essential part of the " sovereignty " they valued so highly

In 1924 and the following years all the European nations, by a Herculean effort, extricated themselves from the quicksands of inflation. They followed, in general, the advice given by a conference summoned by the League of Nations, and to that extent there was a beginning of co-operative action. But there was no effective discussion of the problem as a whole; and nobody suggested the desirability of any common regulative authority to play the part in the new system which the London money-market had informally played in the old.

Every nation accepted without question the view that a return to the Gold Standard was the only way to attain stability, but no provisions were suggested to ensure that it would work. Each nation made its own arrangements: some, like Germany, cancelled their old worthless currency altogether, and made a fresh start; others, like France, kept their old currency, but fixed it to gold at a new value—in the case of France, one-fifth of the old: some, having enough gold for the purpose of " backing " their currency, returned to the Gold Standard proper; others, not having enough gold, decided to use the money of regular gold-standard countries such as America and Britain as backing for their currency, and thus established what was known as the Gold-exchange Standard. There was no uniformity in the new system, and no provision to ensure that it would function freely.

But there were forces already at work which made this impossible. The working of an international monetary system depends largely upon the relations between creditor countries and debtor

87

countries, and these were progressively being dislocated.

Before the war, Britain had been the supreme creditor country of the world, having advanced huge amounts of capital to equip half the world with the implements of modern industry. She had to receive immense annual payments of interest on these investments, and if she had insisted upon being paid in gold, all the gold in the world would have accumulated in her vaults; she would have been throned upon stacks of yellow metal, which would have been of no use to her, and the whole trading and monetary system of the world would have been disorganised. Being a free-trade country, however, she had always accepted payment in goods from her debtors; and she had always reinvested the greater part of the interest she received, thus keeping this wealth continually productive.

During the war, however, much of Britain's foreign holdings had to be sacrificed, though she was still a great creditor country. And during and since the war, America—previously a debtor country —had become a creditor country on an immense scale. But America was a high protectionist country, bent on keeping out foreign goods. This meant that her tariffs made it as difficult as possible for her debtors to pay her in goods; and, as the only alternative was payment in gold, a large part of the world's gold supply had already accumulated in her vaults. It is true that America was still lending abroad upon a colossal scale—if she had not done so, the whole system would have collapsed, as it ultimately did in 1929 and the following years, when she stopped lending. But the more she lent to other countries, the greater became their difficulty in paying their interest and the greater became the drain of gold to America.

And another factor came to intensify this dangerous process. The enormous burden imposed upon Germany as " reparation " for the sufferings of the war had proved to be beyond her power, but in 1924—shortly before the restoration of the Gold Standard in Europe—the amount to be paid annually had been defined. And in the following years the debts owed by all the allied powers to one another and to America were also fixed. The net result of these arrangements was that Germany was under an obligation to pay huge annual sums, without any commercial return; that Britain by her own desire was to receive from Germany and from her debtor-allies only as much as she was required to pay to America; that Belgium, Italy, and other States were to receive somewhat more from Germany than they were to pay to their creditors; and that France and America were both to receive huge net sums.

All these huge international payments had to be made either in gold or in the money of the creditor country; and the money of the creditor countries could only be obtained by the debtor countries by the sale of their goods in the creditor countries. In other words, payment could only be made in gold or goods. But both France and America were highly protectionist countries, and made it as difficult as possible for the goods of their debtors to get into their ports. Therefore the debtors had

89

to get gold wherever they could by the sale of their goods, and send it to the creditor countries. And as the chief creditors under the reparation and debt system were France and America, the world's gold drained more and more into these two countries, and the difficulty of maintaining the Gold Standard became more and more acute.

Another even more important consequence of this process was that, as the world's gold stock diminished, countries on the Gold Standard had to limit the amount of money they issued, in accordance with the rules. The gold in the French and American vaults was of no use for this purpose, because, if these countries had issued money in proportion to the amount of gold they possessed, they would have had so much money that all their prices would have risen precipitously; while in other countries whose money was restricted in amount by their lack of gold, prices would have fallen (as they actually did) very rapidly, and they would have been able to overleap the French and American tariff walls, and to flood the French and American markets with their goods.

In the world at large, therefore, the effect of the gold shortage (combined with the working of tariffs and other factors) was to reduce all prices very alarmingly, because (money being scarce) many more goods had to be given for a given amount of money.

The final crash came in 1931, when Britain was forced off the Gold Standard. The most fantastic prophecies, inspired by memories of the German inflation, were made as to the probable consequences of this step. They were wholly unfulfilled: the departure from the Gold Standard partly undid the evil results of the exaggerated deflation which the struggle to return to gold had caused; and (until the improvement was first checked and then reversed by the imposition of a tariff) British export trade improved, and her unemployment decreased.

In a very short time half the world had followed Britain off the Gold Standard. None of them has seriously suffered. All of them have found it possible to keep their currencies reasonably stable after their initial decline in values; so that many people have begun to doubt whether, in order to obtain a sound monetary system, it is at all necessary to use gold as its basis and regulator, seeing that this metal can so easily be " cornered," and is in any case not being produced in sufficient quantity to meet the world's needs. It seems clear that the Gold Standard will not work in a tariff-ridden world, in which creditor countries refuse to accept payment in goods for the debts due to them.

It is theoretically possible (though no doubt difficult in practice) to create a sound and stable monetary system without any metallic basis at all. And some have toyed with the notion that if this could be done by agreement between all other countries, while France and America remained on the Gold Standard, the problem of debts and reparations might find an easy solution; for all the yellow metal in the world, deprived of its artificial value, could be allowed to flow freely to France and America, and these countries could rejoice in the spectacle of pyramids of it.

In any case, if gold is again to be used as the basis of the world's money, some means must be found of ensuring that it should always be equitably distributed among the countries of the world according to their needs; otherwise a fresh collapse like the last is certain to come about sooner or later. Fair distribution may prove to be impossible in a tariff-ridden world. And, in any case, since it is unlikely that the directorship of the world's financial system will ever again fall into the hands of any single country, as it fell into the hands of Britain during the nineteenth century, the work will somehow have to be done co-operatively, and some system of international regulation and adjustment will have to be devised.

Whether this will ever be done, or not, depends upon whether the world has learnt the lessons which the last few years have been teaching: the lessons that a stable monetary system is essential if the world is ever to enjoy the well-being which is within its reach; that this cannot be achieved so long as all the nations go on their own way, in the exercise of their irresponsible sovereignty; and that the interdependence of the world makes the peril of monetary confusion infinitely greater than it ever was before.

(c) *The Peril of Social Revolution.*

The economic chaos by which Europe has been afflicted since the war, and America since 1929, and the unemployment, loss, waste and suffering which have resulted from it, have brought into being a far-reaching dissatisfaction with what is

called " the existing social order." It is said that
" capitalism " has failed, and must be replaced;
and since Russia is meanwhile showing us the
spectacle of an alternative system, a planned system
whose supreme aim is the well-being of the mass of
working-people, many are saying to-day that unless
capitalism can pull itself together and conquer the
chaos which it has caused, the world will turn to
Communism, and see whether better results cannot
be attained when the whole process of production
and distribution is undertaken by the State, and
the motive of profit-making is banished. Now this,
as we shall presently show, is a highly illogical
argument. But men are not governed by logic;
and if the failure to grapple with the causes of world
distress is long continued, there may well be violent
upheavals in many countries, inspired by the Russian example.

Our troubles are not due to the breakdown of
capitalism or any other *ism*. They are due to the
failure of the world's governments to recognise and
to act upon the facts of interdependence; and the
ruling oligarchy in Russia is as guilty of this failure
of vision as the other governments, since it has
persuaded itself that it can create an insulated
society in the modern world.

Moreover, it is absurd to describe by such a word
as " capitalism "—as if it were a static system
embodying a definite theory—the incessantly
changing and infinitely various mixture of every
possible form and type of economic organisation
in the midst of which we live. Nowhere in the world
(except perhaps in Russia) is human life ruled by an

ism, or moulded to suit a rigid formula invented by a single dictatorial mind. In our kaleidoscopic world there are many small concerns still which are managed by the owners of the capital invested in them; many more which are owned by one set of people and managed by another set; some (like the railways) in which private ownership is qualified by a very high degree of State regulation; others which are conducted by statutory authorities, and forbidden to make profits; others which are owned by co-operative societies; others which are owned and managed directly by the State or by municipalities; and all of them, even the freest, are subject in many respects to the control and supervision of the State. Such a various and changing complex of different forms cannot be described by the word " capitalism " or any other *ism*, because it is not the expression of any single rigid theory; it is the expression of a free society, experimenting with every method of organisation that seems to promise some form of success.

By whatever name we call them, the methods of wealth-production which are at work in our world have certainly not failed in their primary function of producing wealth. In this they have been immeasurably more successful than the Russian methods—otherwise we should not be complaining of over-production. They can produce, and are producing, enough to make the whole world prosperous. The failure has not been in regard to production, but in regard to the distribution of the wealth produced; and this, as John Stuart Mill long ago pointed out, is the sphere in which States and governments can most usefully intervene in the economic process. It is the distribution of the world's wealth that has gone wrong; and inefficiency in distribution is reacting on production by making it unprofitable.

We have already discussed in this chapter two ways in which the governments of the world—not the organisers of production—have fallen short. They have, with their tariffs and other restrictions, prevented the world's wealth from flowing freely from country to country; and they have failed to perform successfully one of the essential functions of governments at all times—the creation of a monetary system which will make the interchange of goods and services easy, just and secure, between man and man and between country and country.

But more than this is required if the distribution of the world's wealth to the world's inhabitants is to be carried out successfully. It is necessary, first, to ensure that the right proportions are maintained between spending and saving; secondly, to ensure that wealth is justly shared among those who help to produce it, in proportion to the value of their contributions, and in such a way as not only to reward but to stimulate effort; thirdly, to ensure that the processes of production are not ruthless in the treatment of their instruments, and that in a rich and civilised society nobody shall suffer undeserved and degrading penury; and, fourthly, to ensure that an adequate proportion of the wealth produced is made available for those social and intellectual activities without which our civilisation must be a mean and sordid thing. Until comparatively

95

recently, we have been accustomed to assume that these functions were no part of the duty of governments, but could be left to the spontaneous action of individuals. From that view the whole world has now departed, and there is no government which does not make some sort of attempt to meet most of these needs, and which does not annex for this purpose a substantial share of the wealth enjoyed by its citizens. But we have scarcely even now begun to realise thàt these functions of a civilised community demand international as well as national action; and social health throughout the world must suffer unless these needs are internationally as well as nationally considered.

Take first the distribution of wealth between saving and spending. It is now pretty widely agreed that the alternate booms and slumps which are so marked and so unfortunate a feature of our economic life are largely due to maladjustment between the use of wealth for capital purposes (saving) and its use for immediate consumption. When trade is thriving, there is a tendency on the part of manufacturers to undertake large capital expansions to meet the growing demand; this involves increased employment in the constructional industries, and therefore, for a time, an enlargement of purchasing power. But the point soon arrives when the mechanism of production is too great for the available demand, and production ceases to be profitable. Then the slump begins; there is growing unemployment, especially in the constructional trades, which leads to reduced purchases of consumable goods. Now it is possible to think out methods whereby the expenditure on capital works might be to some extent evened out, with the result of evening out also the purchasing power of the people. But it is of little use to apply these methods in one country alone, because in our interdependent world neither booms nor slumps are ever limited to a single country. The problem is one which demands common planning and concurrent action. Interdependence has thus greatly increased the difficulty of dealing with the alternation of booms and slumps which is one of the most unhealthy features of our economic life.

The second, and perhaps the most vital, aspect of the problem of distribution is that of reducing the gross and crying disparities between great wealth and great poverty which have resulted from modern industrialism, and which do more than anything else to create discontent and therefore to discourage effort. Whatever methods may be used for this purpose—the steady increase of wage-rates, the development of profit-sharing schemes, the use of taxation as a means of equalisation, the wider diffusion of ownership rights (and all of these have their value)—it must be obvious that it is difficult for one country to carry this sort of policy very far, in an interdependent world, without placing itself (or seeming to place itself) at a disadvantage in the competition with other countries. This was recognised in the institution of the new international system at the end of the war; and the International Labour Office was established for the express purpose of enabling the nations to march in step in the amelioration of the conditions of life of working people. It has not yet achieved much success; nor is it likely to do so, so long as the nations regard international trade as a form of international war.

It is in the fixation of hours of work, with a view to the increase of leisure, that the I.L.O. has come nearest to success, having drafted an Eight-hours Convention which many nations have accepted. The problem of leisure is likely in the future to be even more important than the problem of pay. As things now are, the rapid progress of mechanism and of mass-production methods is one of the principal causes of unemployment, whereas it ought to be the means of enabling the mass of working folk to give less of their time to livelihood and more to living. But here, again, rapid progress in the shortening of working hours is not easy for any one country in an interdependent world; the nations must somehow learn to act in concert if we are to see the better distribution of leisure which may be at once the best way of sharing the well-being that is now within reach of mankind, and the best way of alleviating unemployment, which is the ugliest feature of our industrial life.

The third aspect of sound distribution—the maintenance of healthy conditions of work, and the prevention of needless suffering among the workers and their dependants—has been carried much farther in Britain than in any other country; but it is significant that British employers regard themselves as being hampered by these provisions in their fight for a share of world trade. In America the development of a sound system of factory-law and of social insurance has been very seriously retarded by the fact that these subjects are within the province of the forty-eight State legislatures; and any proposal for reform in any State always has to meet the plausible criticism that, however sound in itself, the proposal will place the industries of the State at a disadvantage in comparison with those of other States. The nations of the inter-dependent world are in the same position in relation to one another as the States of the American Union: none of them can, or at any rate few of them will, make the progress that is practicable and found to be necessary, unless all the rest are willing to move in the same direction. Here, again, interdependence, in the absence of any adequate common machinery, is actually an obstacle to needed progress.

Finally, if our civilisation is to be worth while, it must provide, out of its potentially illimitable resources, the means for affording to all its citizens the opportunities of securing good houses and health-ful conditions of life, the opportunity through education of making the most of their own powers, and the chance of enjoying the best that they are able to appreciate in thought, letters, music and the fine arts. All this, in our complex modern world, is only possible by a diversion of wealth to these ends on a great scale by State action. But expenditure on these purposes, the highest and the most re-munerative to which wealth can be devoted, is apt to be denounced as mere waste, handicapping the nation in the fierce rivalry of trade. There is no field in which " economy " (in the mean sense of parsimony) is more clamantly demanded; and this even in those aspects (not the highest) that actually help to increase the productive efficiency of the community. The interdependence of our world is thus used as an argument against progress; and is likely to be so used until our world has somehow equipped itself with the organs necessary to enable it to make interdependence the stimulus to a co-operative advance in well-being, and until the nations have learnt to regard their relations as those, not of conflict, but of mutual protection and mutual aid. Perhaps the day will come when the nations will agree not only upon a maximum proportion of each nation's income which should be spent upon the implements of destruction, but upon a minimum proportion of each nation's income which should be spent upon the instruments of creation; but for the present this is no more than a Utopian dream.

It appears, then, that an interdependent 'world of sovereign nations is a very dangerous and a very insecure world. Interdependence makes war more difficult to avoid, and more ruinous if it comes. It makes the extension of the national spirit over the world —though in itself a fine thing—the source of grim anticipations for the future. It makes the long-established habit of the nations of striving after economic self-sufficiency by way of tariffs a source of mere ruin to them all. 'It makes the establishment of a sound monetary system more necessary than ever, but also more difficult than ever. It makes the problem of justly distributing the wealth which the world can now produce in unprecedented abundance more complex than ever.

Plainly the world has reached a stage in its development which is of supreme importance, and which must make calls upon the wisdom, foresight and forbearance of its statesmen greater than they have had to meet in any earlier age. In this year 1932, the world's statesmen are just beginning to appreciate the magnitude of the problem that lies before them.

Meanwhile it is for us all, in a democratic era, to be striving to think out these problems as best we can. We must ask ourselves, first, what are the necessary consequences of interdependence, and what changes must be made in the organisation of human society if it is to be a source not of ruin but of blessing to mankind. And we must ask ourselves, secondly, whether the political machinery of the modern world, both national and international, is of such a kind as to promise us (what we have not yet enjoyed) the right kind of leadership at this turning-point in human history.

These will be the themes of the remaining chapters in this little book.

CHAPTER IV

THE NECESSARY CONSEQUENCES OF INTERDEPENDENCE

A. *The Limitation of State Sovereignty.*

THE irresistible conclusion of our analysis is that the world is being brought to ruin because the condition of interdependence into which it has been brought is incompatible with the exercise of unlimited sovereignty by the nations included within it, and with the ideal of self-sufficiency which they are all tempted to pursue. If ruin is to be averted, either the interdependence of the world must be brought to an end (which is what the nations seem to be striving after), or the sovereignty of the nations must somehow be limited, or its exercise restrained.

It is as impossible to stop the growing advance of the world towards fuller interdependence as it would be to stop the movement of the tides. It could only be done by a return to the conditions of barbarism, by a deliberate abandonment of modern methods of production and communication; and the development of these things is being eagerly pressed forward by all nations at the very time when they are struggling against its consequences!

We are therefore driven to inquire whether unlimited sovereignty is a necessary attribute of free

States; and whether sovereignty, or certain elements in it, might not be limited, or pooled, without impairing, but rather strengthening, the real freedom of States.

I. *The Doctrine of Sovereignty.*

This brings us to the consideration of a doctrine of jurisprudence, or political theory, which has long been regarded as fundamental. It may seem that an abstract theory, of which the ordinary citizen has never heard, can have very little bearing upon the eminently practical problems with which we are concerned. But theories have a much greater influence upon men's conduct than is often admitted; and no political theory has ever exercised a greater influence upon the course of political action than the doctrine of sovereignty. It is drilled into the mind of every lawyer in every country, as one of the axioms of his science; and lawyers play a great part in the government of every country. It is treated as an axiom in almost every treatise on political science, and implied in almost every history; and there are still some politicians who have learnt a little history and a little political science, while those who lack this equipment are apt to be deferential to those who possess it. For these reasons the doctrine of sovereignty has wielded an extraordinary influence upon the policy of nations—all the more so because its teaching harmonises with the instinctive pride of nationality.

Briefly stated, the doctrine of sovereignty is that in every State there must somewhere reside a definite, recognisable, unlimited and indivisible power, from which all lesser powers within the State derive their authority, and which all the citizens of the State habitually obey. If no such supreme power exists, then the State will not be truly a State, and will dissolve into anarchy. This supreme power cannot be divided, and it must not be subject to any limitation, either from within or from without the State, for in that case it will not be " sovereign "— sovereignty will belong to the power which can limit it. If the supreme power is controlled or limited by any external authority, the real sovereignty belongs to this external authority, which will be a Super-State.

Such is the theory in which all public men in the Western world have been bred for four centuries, and which has led them to regard any restriction or limitation of sovereignty as an intolerable and dangerous undermining of the very foundations of our common life. What is the basis of this theory? How did it come to wield such a power over the minds of men? Does it correspond with the actual facts? Or is it a fundamental misreading of the facts, and are the arguments which are based upon it dangerously misleading?

These are very important questions. And it is highly significant that—just at the time when the doctrine of sovereignty, in its practical applications, is producing very dangerous consequences—modern political thought is beginning seriously to question the validity of this doctrine, and to contend that it springs from a very dangerous misreading of the nature of human relationships in organised societies.

How did this doctrine arise? The mind of man

appears instinctively to assume that there must be an ultimate authority responsible for whatever happens. Just as his mental make-up almost compels him to believe in an omnipotent God controlling the universe, so in his own affairs he likes to believe that there is an ultimate authority beyond which there is no appeal. Mediæval thinkers believed that there *must* be a supreme vicegerent of God on earth; and they found him either in the Pope or the Emperor, or in the two jointly. It did not matter that neither Pope nor Emperor was able in fact to exercise effective supremacy: the mediæval mind readily accepted such contradictions between theory and practice. Roman law, as set forth in the Institutes and Codes of Justinian, which were eagerly studied in the Middle Ages, reinforced this belief with its assumption that the Emperor was the source of all law, and therefore absolute sovereign.

When the mediæval era came to an end in the Renascence and the Reformation, and the political supremacy of Empire and Papacy were alike discarded, both political and religious thinkers felt the need of defining where ultimate authority now lay; and both Machiavelli and Luther found it in the ruling prince of each State, whose sovereignty was held to include not only the laying down of laws, but even the determination of the beliefs of their subjects. When France was torn asunder by the wars of religion, Bodin seized upon the doctrine, and gave to it its modern form; it did indeed appear, in that time of unending civil strife, that a State was threatened with dissolution unless it was unified by a central sovereign power which everybody obeyed. Hobbes still further developed the theory under the challenge of civil disorder in England, and his statement of it has ever since been of classic authority. Used at first by despots to justify their despotism, the doctrine of sovereignty was later applied as a buttress for the authority of Parliaments; and Dicey found one of the great merits of the British Constitution in the fact that (in his view) it quite clearly and unmistakably concentrated undivided sovereignty upon Parliament, which (in the favourite phrase of the text-books) " can do everything except turn a man into a woman." The doctrine came to be universally accepted, as an unchallengeable axiom; nearly all the great writers on jurisprudence, such as our own Austin, made it the very pivot of their teaching. And the whole world took it for granted that a State was not fully a State unless its government, whatever its form might be, enjoyed full " sovereignty "—absolute authority over all lesser powers within its jurisdiction, and over all its individual citizens; and absolute freedom from any control by any external power.

Yet this respectable doctrine, which has wielded such unchallenged authority, is mere words, and has no relation to reality.

If we ask ourselves, for example, where this essential sovereign power is to be found in the United States of America (to which nobody will deny the character of a powerful State), the answer is, that it cannot be identified. Neither the President nor Congress is " sovereign," because the powers of both are definitely limited by the Constitution. The legislatures and Governors of the forty-eight States are still more obviously not sovereign, though they wield certain sovereign powers which nobody can legally take from them. Is the Constitution sovereign? It is absurd to attribute these powers to a piece of paper. Is the Supreme Court sovereign? It interprets the Constitution, and can disallow any acts of the President, of Congress, or of any State which infringe that document; but it only interprets, it cannot *act*, as a sovereign power must do. Or does sovereign power reside in those who can alter the Constitution—a majority of two-thirds in three-quarters of the separate States? In that case, the sovereign power is singularly inaccessible and difficult to bring into operation!

Even in Britain, with all respect to Mr. Dicey, the sovereign power (if it exists) is not easily identified. He assigns it to Parliament. But Parliament wields almost no real power: it is the creature of the cabinet, and of the caucus of the party that happens to obtain a majority of seats.

Even if we could identify the seat of sovereignty, can we pretend, with any loyalty to the facts, that the sovereign power is absolute and unlimited even within the boundary of the State? Suppose a Parliament to be elected in Britain with a majority of reactionary Conservatives—a not wholly unimaginable possibility—could it, in the exercise of its sovereign power, abolish all Trade Unions? On paper it could; but in fact it certainly could not. Can it be pretended (as the theory of sovereignty assumes) that all the Churches owe their authority to the sovereign power, which could deprive them of it? They owe their authority to the convictions

107

and the loyalty of their members, just as the State does; and if the State, in a moment of madness, were to attempt to suppress all Churches, the " habitual obedience " which its subjects owe to it would fail, and there would be a clash of loyalties, in which the State, despite all its power, would get the worst, because it would have overstrained the loyalty of its subjects, from which it draws its strength.

It would appear, then, that the power which the State wields over its subjects is, in fact, neither absolute nor unlimited. It depends upon the loyalty of its subjects, and will reach its limits when it overstrains this loyalty. The limit will be more quickly reached with an intelligent and freedom-loving people than with others; that is why the democratic system, which provides for periodic judgments upon the action of the sovereign body, and periodic replacements of its personnel, is the only practicable method of government for a highly developed State.

In truth, the sovereignty of the ruling body in the State differs only in degree, not in kind, from the power wielded over their members by the authorised rulers of spontaneously formed groups, such as Churches or Trade Unions. The source of authority, in each case, is the loyalty of the members, and these loyalties may sometimes clash—there have been occasions upon which both Trade Unions and Churches have defied the State, not without success. In each case the source of this loyalty is the conviction that the moral and physical well-being of the members is served by the body to which loyalty is given. If this conviction is weakened or destroyed, loyalty also will be weakened or destroyed: the Trade

Union will lose its members, the Church will become derelict, and the ruling power in each case will not be obeyed. The same fate may befall the State—and *has* befallen many States in history; for the State, as much as the Trade Union, was made for man, not man for the State. And if the belief grows (as it is beginning to grow) that, by insisting upon absolute sovereignty and self-sufficiency *vis-à-vis* other States, the State is failing to serve the moral and physical well-being of its members, then the loyalty of the subjects, and the power of the rulers, will diminish until this dangerous claim to sovereignty and this vicious struggle for self-sufficiency are qualified.

It is, of course, true that the difference in *degree* between the loyalty due to the State (and therefore the power wielded by it), and the loyalty due to other organisations, is very great indeed; but it is still only a difference in degree, and the assertion (implicit in the doctrine of sovereignty) that the claim of the State is altogether different in *kind* and is fundamental, and that its power is therefore so unqualified as to be properly described by the special name of " sovereignty," cannot stand the test of examination. A good citizen will hesitate long, and rightly, before he defies the power of the State, or refuses to obey it; he will hesitate not only because it wields tremendous powers, and not only because it is reinforced by the emotion of patriotism, but also and above all because the interests which it protects and the needs which it serves are so much greater, and range so much more widely, than those of any other human organisation. But in our era it begins to be apparent that some of these interests and some of these needs cannot adequately be served by any State in isolation, but demand co-operation between many States. And as this conviction grows and spreads, the most powerful of States may find that they are only able to ensure the loyalty upon which their power rests if they are willing to play their part in a collective system which can alone meet these needs, and if, in order to do so, they are willing to forgo the unlimited sovereignty which they have been accustomed to claim.

In regard to its external aspect the doctrine of unlimited State sovereignty is no less out of relation with the facts than in regard to its internal aspect. It must be obvious that no State can do exactly as it likes, without running serious risks : this is true of the greatest as well as the smallest of States. In accordance with the doctrine of sovereignty, States may claim in theory the right always to be the judges in their own cause; but they will seldom venture to exercise it in practice. They will only deliberately resort to war for the enforcement of their claims if they can persuade themselves that they are likely to win, for the cost of defeat is always—and especially in modern conditions—vastly greater than the value of any claim which can be made the cause of war. Every State knows that, if it earns the name of being a reckless disturber of the peace, it will have to count upon the hostility of other States, which will cause it heavy loss even if it does not take the form of military opposition.

In other words, the supposed unrestricted sovereignty of States is in a high degree qualified, even in

the case of the strongest, by the necessity of considering the opinions of other States. The will of the
civilised world as a whole has always been stronger
than the will of the most powerful of States, as
Spain, France and Germany have each discovered
at the moments of their greatest strength. The
" external sovereignty," which (according to the
doctrine we are examining) is an inherent and
inalienable attribute of statehood, is in fact definitely
limited already, and in the case of all but a few of
the most powerful, very narrowly restricted, by the
overriding though as yet unorganised sovereignty of
the civilised world as a whole. And any exercise
of it is, as experience has shown, attended by so
many risks and uncertainties that a clearer definition
of the spheres within which the exercise of sovereignty
is debarred by the will of the civilised world would
be to the advantage of all States.

There are many States whose external sovereignty
is limited, not only in fact, but in form. Of these
the most outstanding examples are the States of the
British Empire, which is the despair of the theorists
of sovereignty. Is Canada a sovereign State? Her
citizens " habitually obey " the government of
Canada, and no other. But the final judgment on
some of the law-cases in which they are concerned is
given by an imperial court sitting in London; their
Constitution was enacted, and (in theory at all
events) can only be amended, by the Imperial
Parliament; and they have been, and may again
be, involved in war by the action of Britain. It is
true that this state of things could immediately be
terminated by an Act of the Canadian Parliament

declaring Canada independent, and that Britain neither would nor could resist such a decision. But this would involve a breach by the Canadians of a loyalty which they value—a loyalty not merely to Britain, but to the whole loose group of free States known as the British Commonwealth; and this breach would probably (unless great provocation had been offered) weaken the loyalty of the Canadians to their own government, and thereby impair the sovereignty of that government. Are we then to say (in accordance with our rigid doctrine) that since Canada is not " sovereign," sovereignty must belong to the external power that can limit it—either to Britain, or to the whole British Commonwealth? But that is nonsense: the government of Britain, still more the non-existent government of the British Empire, is not " habitually obeyed " by the Canadians, and does not wield absolute power over the subordinate ruling powers in Canada. Where, then, is the sovereign power in Canada to be found?

The answer would seem to be that, in the case of Canada, and indeed in the cases of all the States of the British Empire, including the dependent colonies, not to mention the cases of many other States, the supposedly " indivisible " powers of sovereignty are in fact divided. They are divided in very different proportions in different cases: in the case of Canada, very few of the powers of sovereignty are withheld from the government of Canada, while in the case of Nigeria or Kenya, the most important of these powers are withheld. So it would appear that, despite the theorists, the powers of sovereignty are not in fact indivisible, and are in fact often divided.

This has long since been clear in the United States, of whose Constitution the central idea is the division of sovereign powers—between the Federal Government on the one hand, and the States on the other; and again between the President and Congress, and between the Governor and the Assembly in each State; and the Supreme Court exists to ensure that this division of sovereignty is never impaired. The division was carried out in the eighteenth century in a rather rigid way, which did not foresee the changing needs of a later time, and on this ground it has been criticised by Dicey and other doctrinaires of sovereignty. But the important thing is that, though the division may sometimes have worked cumbrously, it *has* worked. The United States has not been reduced to anarchy, as, according to the doctrine of sovereignty, it ought to have been. Sovereignty *can* be divided; some elements of it *can* be withheld from States which are in other respects sovereign; and these withheld powers *can* be pooled, and exercised in the common interest of all. There may well be differences of opinion as to which rights of sovereignty can, and which cannot, effectively be wielded in common. But there can be no doubt at all that it is *possible* to divide sovereign rights, and to pool some of them for common exercise by a number of co-operating States.

The doctrine of sovereignty, as it has been preached from the time of Bodin and Hobbes to the time of Austin and Dicey, is a mere abstraction which has no relation to the realities, and which may have, and often has had, a very mischievous influence—never more mischievous than to-day.

II. *The Dream of a World-State.*

There could be no clearer illustration of the influence of the doctrine of sovereignty, or of the loose thinking which it has encouraged, than the fact that it is widely assumed, by men of very different schools of thought, that the only practicable alternative to the continuance of a multitude of States each claiming unlimited sovereignty is the establishment of a single vast Super-State, or World-State.

When the League of Nations was instituted, the criticism most often levelled against it was the assertion that it was meant to be a Super-State; and this was felt to be so damaging that the authors of the League insisted that it would not involve any limitation of the sovereignty of its members, although they must have been perfectly aware that it would be merely futile unless it did so. Strangely enough, it was in America, the classic example of divided or partitioned sovereignty, that this criticism was most loudly heard; and the main reason why America refused to join the League was precisely that it would be a Super-State, overriding the inalienable and indivisible sovereignty of the United States—which is already divided.

On the other side, the League has been criticised, by impatient idealists like Mr H. G. Wells, precisely because it is not, and does not pretend to be, the World-State of their dreams. They have no patience with the slow and tedious debates of the League Assembly and Council, which seem to be nothing more than a new arena for the old rivalries and intrigues. They point with scorn to twelve years wasted over the discussion of disarmament, without any progress at all. The League is not a power above all governments, exercising sovereignty over the whole world: it *consists* of the governments, and is impotent unless they all agree; even when they all agree on the policy to be pursued, the League itself can do nothing, but must wait for all the separate governments to take action on the agreed lines, at their own time and in their own way. This is, in the view of these impatient idealists, precisely where the League is wrong, precisely why the League can never be of any use.

Profoundly impressed by the interdependence of the world, they want to see this interdependence reflected in a single powerful organisation, to which all the existing States shall be as definitely subordinate as are the forty-eight American States to the Union. They want to see a World-State, equipped with an army powerful enough to enforce its will and to maintain absolute peace throughout the world: it should be the only army in the world, apart from the mere police-forces which the member-States may be licensed to maintain. They want this World-State to maintain a single currency for the whole world, to abolish all tariffs throughout the world, to regulate the powerful international industrial combines which more and more tend to dominate the world's productive activities, to create a single citizenship of the world, and perhaps a single legal system. Probably no single writer has set forth all these claims as essential parts of the better order which the World-State is to create; certainly, so far as the writer is aware, nobody has yet attempted to work out, even in outline, the structure of the World-State, or to indicate by what means it is to be established. But all these functions have been advocated as necessary for an efficient world-order, and as only possible if provided by a World-State.

Those who speak and write in these terms are, in fact, enslaved by the very doctrine of sovereignty against which they protest. They cling to the superstition that sovereignty must be one, indivisible and irresistible. They have returned to the dreams of mediæval thinkers like Dante, who could not be content unless there were a single vicegerent of God for the governance of the world, and who regarded the strivings of nations towards statehood as a wholly evil thing. They habitually denounce, not merely the excesses or exaggerations of nationalism, but the national spirit in itself, as a device of the devil, and, like Lessing, regard patriotism as a vice. They are *cosmopolitans*, not *internationalists*.

If it be true that the assertion of the rights of unlimited sovereignty by every Nation-State is impracticable in an interdependent world, it is equally true that the creation, as an alternative, of a single dominating World-State is also impracticable. And since a great deal of sloppy thinking is being encouraged, and a great deal of prejudice created, by loose talk about the World-State as the supreme object of loyalty and endeavour, it is desirable at once to clear the ground by setting forth briefly *why* the idea of a World-State is impracticable, and would be intolerable if it could be realised.

It is impracticable, to begin with, because there must be arrayed against it the most powerful thing in the world—the force of national sentiment. It is conceivable that the nations might be willing to forgo or pool certain *elements* of their sovereignty, in the hope of making their freedom more secure; but it is inconceivable that they should forgo potentially all their sovereign powers, and thus wholly sacrifice their freedom and independence by setting up over themselves a power which, *ex hypothesi*, is to exercise unlimited sovereignty. Even those who regard the national spirit as wholly vicious must at the least recognise that it is a very formidable fact, which cannot be brushed aside; and that it must preclude the possibility of a World-State in any intelligible sense of that term.

It is impracticable, secondly, because it is impossible to imagine any political structure which would be capable of including within itself all the infinitely various races and peoples of mankind. The contrasts between them are too great; and the possibilities of intrigue, corruption and abuse of power in such a system are beyond imagination. The real master of such a State would be the commander of its army; he would very easily make himself the Lord of the World; and the government of the World-State would soon come to resemble that of the Roman Empire—a tyranny, put up to auction at intervals by the Prætorian Guard, with an impotent Senate in the background.

It is impracticable, thirdly, because a World-State could not possibly win from its subjects that impassioned loyalty which is the strength of the Nation-States and the source of their sovereignty, and which alone enables them to overcome the lesser loyalties of little local States, with their petty wars and their tariffs. It may perhaps be argued that such a loyalty would grow up in time, when the World-State had established itself. That would in any case depend upon the success with which it achieved its tremendous task; and when we realise how difficult it is to secure justice and efficiency in the government even of States of reasonable size and homogeneous character, the possibility of attaining, in a single world-government, such a degree of success as would command unquestioning loyalty and prevent the people of any country from feeling that they were being unfairly treated, must appear utterly beyond hope. In any case, as we have seen, one of the main sources of the loyalty which is the strength of Nation-States arises from the sense of difference from other nations. There could be no such feeling in a World-State. A World-State would lack the cement by which great aggregates of people can be held together.

It will be said that the World-State will, of course, not be what is called a " unitary " State, but a " federal " State—what the Germans call a *Bundes-staat*. But it is of the essence of a Federal State that, while each of the federated members reserves certain powers, the federal powers which are placed under common control are wielded by a government which is directly representative of the whole population within the federal area, is constituted in proportion to numbers, and exercises direct authority over all the individual citizens. No such system is practicable for the world as a whole, or is ever likely to be practicable.

The only possible alternative is what the Germans call a *Staatenbund*, or League of States, in which the agreed common powers are wielded by a group of representatives of the governments of the member-States, who exercise no direct authority over individual citizens. But a *Staatenbund* is not a State at all, in any intelligible sense of the term: it is an alliance of States; possibly a very close alliance, but still only an alliance or league, and its effective action is conditioned by the readiness of its members to act in common. It was precisely on this basis that the League of Nations was designed. Its inspiring idea is, not that of displacing, overriding or controlling its member-States; but that of enabling them to perform in co-operation those functions of the State which in modern conditions cannot be efficiently performed except in co-operation.

The enthusiasts for the idea of a World-State dislike the League of Nations for the same reason which led the enthusiasts for German unity in the early nineteenth century to dislike the Germanic Confederation of 1815—because it is a *Staatenbund*, and not a *Bundesstaat*; and because it is therefore not a step towards, but an obstacle in the way of, the formation of a single unified State. The Germans of 1820 were right in their dislike of the *Staatenbund*, because Germany was capable of becoming a united federal State. The Utopians of 1930 are wrong in their dislike of the League of Nations, because the world as a whole is *not* capable, and probably never will be capable, of becoming a single State, not even a *Bundesstaat*.

The League of Nations may hitherto have been

ineffective. Its powers may be inadequate; its organisation may be deficient. These things can be altered if opinion in the member-States wishes that they should be altered. But the essential principle upon which the League has been constituted is sound. The common needs and interests of the interdependent world cannot be served by setting up a sovereign Super-State in control of all the existing States. That idea is only an illustration of the loose, unreal, abstract thinking which has been encouraged by the general acceptance of the doctrine of sovereignty. These needs can only be met by the organised co-operation of free States, each abandoning or pooling certain elements of its sovereignty in order to enjoy the rest in greater freedom.

But this conclusion brings us to two further questions. What are the elements of sovereignty, now claimed and (in form rather than fact) enjoyed by the Nation-States, which ought to be either limited or pooled? And by what machinery should these pooled powers be exercised? Have we yet found, in the working of the League and its associated organs, the right machinery?

III. *What Elements of Sovereignty must be Limited?*

What, then, are the elements of sovereignty which ought to be pooled and exercised jointly on behalf of all States, or limited in some other way?

Clearly they are those which relate to functions of government which, in modern conditions, no State can perform for and by itself. States exist in order to render to their citizens certain essential services which the citizens cannot supply for themselves.

Two of the most essential of these are (*a*) the provision of security against internal disorder and external attack; and (*b*) the provision of the conditions in which the citizen can earn his livelihood, and be reasonably certain of getting a just return for his efforts. In an interdependent world, neither of these essential services can be fully performed by any State which trusts to its own resources alone.

So far as internal security is concerned, each State can, or ought to, do all that is required. If and in so far as it fails, this is because it is a badly governed State; but that is its own concern, and ought to be amended by the action of the citizens themselves. It may indeed happen that for one reason or another —its size, its traditions, its lack of real unity—a State proves to be quite incapable of obtaining security within its own limits (a condition of things which seems almost to have been reached in modern China). In such a case, it may in the long run be necessary for another State, or a group of States, or the whole Society of Nations, to intervene for the purpose of restoring order. But intervention of this sort is a last resource, which ought to be used very reluctantly; and since, if undertaken by any single State (as by Japan in China), it may cause dangerous international friction, it would be best that such intervention, when necessary, should be undertaken under the joint auspices of the nations.

This has never hitherto been possible. The restoration of order in India, in Egypt, in Morocco, and in other instances was, in fact, undertaken by individual States, inspired by very mixed motives. It is significant, indeed, that in the more recent instances of Egypt and Morocco the Great Powers insisted upon international consultation and approval —an evidence of the growing interdependence of the world. The institution of the League of Nations provides, for the first time, the machinery whereby this procedure can be regularised, and brought under the ægis of the civilised world as a whole. The offence of Japan in 1931 was that she disregarded this fact. Since all nations are, or can become, members of the League, it is likely, as it is certainly desirable, that future interventions in the internal affairs of any State should only take place with the approval, and under the ægis, of the League. The nation which has fallen into anarchy may itself invite intervention in these conditions. China, for example, might well ask for the help of the League in restoring political order, as Austria asked for its help in restoring financial stability. Once the prestige of the League is fully established, it is safe to assume that it will be resorted to for such purposes; and if or when this practice becomes established, the most fruitful pretext for imperialist aggressions, and one of the greatest dangers of war, will have been removed.

But common action of this sort, for the restoration of order within the limits of a particular State, must be very rare, and very reluctantly employed. Normally every State must be regarded as fully capable of, and solely responsible for, the protection of its citizens against internal disorder.

The case of protection against external attack is far different. In the conditions of modern war no country, not the most powerful, can by its own power give to its citizens security against attack, and against attack in forms of unimaginable cruelty and horror; the exposure of the mass of ordinary citizens to the worst atrocities being one of the inevitable consequences of the application of science to the arts of destruction. There are very few countries that could even make themselves secure, in the event of war, against a ruin more absolute and irremediable than has ever visited any country in the past. No country, therefore, can by its own strength perform one of the most essential functions for which the State exists. In order to perform its proper work, every State must depend upon co-operative action; and therefore this is a sphere in which it is vital for the future of civilisation that the sovereignty claimed by the nations should be limited or pooled. If the nations wish for security, they must resign their exclusive responsibility for obtaining it.

The second sphere in which it is now impossible for any national government, by its own strength alone, to perform one of its essential functions, is the economic sphere.

No nation can organise, in isolation, a monetary system which will enable the operations of trade to be carried on successfully. Yet the right of coinage, that is to say, the right of controlling the issue of money, has always been one of the elements of sovereignty to which governments have most firmly clung. It has become abundantly clear that some limitation or pooling of *this* sovereign right is indispensable. The nations have already recognised this in practice; when they all linked their currencies to gold, they accepted a certain limitation of their freedom of action. But experience has demonstrated that more than this is necessary. They must somehow contrive to agree upon some common machinery for the regulation of the world's monetary system.

Again, it is clear that tariffs have (as the Geneva Conference of 1927 recognised) ceased to be merely the concern of the individual States that establish them, and have become a common international concern. It is needful not only that the absurd tariffs of to-day, which are bringing international trade to a standstill, should be reduced, but that in some way future extravagances of this kind should be restrained by agreement. This must necessarily be a slow process; it can only make progress in proportion as the nations abandon the false aim of self-sufficiency, which they will be slow to do.

Yet again, the vast industrial combines, operating in every part of the world, which are a feature of our modern economic order, must be subjected to some sort of regulation, if they are not to be made the means of plundering consumers everywhere in the interests of small groups of monopolists. No country has yet found effective means of regulating its own monopolies without unduly restraining trade. They must take counsel together, and act in common, not only in regard to this, but in regard to many other needs of international commerce. The United States, in which all questions of commercial law are within the powers of the various States, has found it necessary to set up an Inter-State Commerce Commission. The world as a whole will have to feel its way towards a similar co-operative system of regulation.

There are many other matters in which a developed system of common regulation will be found essential as the interdependence of the world increases, and in regard to some of them a substantial degree of co-operation already exists in practice. For example, there is no reason why the laws of citizenship and naturalisation should not be made more uniform; or why the passport systems of all countries and their rules in regard to transit by road, rail, sea and air—including rules devised to secure the safety of the traveller—should not be harmonised; or why the patent laws of all countries should not be assimilated; or why there should not be more effective co-operation in the suppression of crime and the extradition of criminals—a sphere in which there is already some degree of co-operation; or why the war against disease, and especially against transmissible diseases, should not be an organised, co-operative war, as in some degree it already is. In all these matters, and in many others, pressure of facts will enforce organised co-operation, and will necessitate the creation of machinery to make this co-operation effective.

But every act of co-operation involves, in a greater or less degree, an abrogation of sovereignty on the part of the States concerned—a voluntary abandonment of the right of each co-operating State to do as it likes, in order to obtain advantages which it could not obtain by isolated action. And there is no use pretending that this is not so, as supporters of the League of Nations have sometimes attempted to do.

Nor is the limitation or pooling of sovereignty a wholly new and unheard-of idea. It is already practised: the indivisible is already divided. When the nations formed an International Postal Union, they all forwent one minute portion of their sovereign rights; when they accepted the Copyright Convention, they forwent another portion.

To-day the nations are called upon to forgo or to limit elements in their sovereignty which are far more important than these, and which they have always regarded as vital:—the right of war, and of being the judges in their own cause; the right of coinage, and of exercising irresponsible control over their own monetary systems; the right of trade-regulation, including tariffs. Will the pressure of necessity be strong enough to make them give way on these great matters? That is the greatest question of our time. Will they succeed in working out methods of co-operation in these matters which, while necessarily involving some limitation of their sovereignty, will not weaken but strengthen their freedom to live their own lives in their own way? That question can only be solved by experiment; and we must therefore try to determine, in each of the three most important cases (war, money and trade-regulation), what devices are practicable, short of the establishment of a sovereign Super-State.

CHAPTER V

B. *The Abolition of War.*

THE establishment of a collective system of security
is the first and the greatest task of an interdependent
world; the essential foundation of mutual confidence
and co-operation in other spheres.

I. *The League of Nations and Its Projects.*

This has already been recognised, at any rate in
form, by all the nations of the world. They have
all, in principle, abandoned their right to go to
war whenever they think fit, their claim to be the
only judges in their own cause. All members of
the League of Nations have pledged themselves,
under the Covenant, never to go to war until they
have exhausted all the means of averting war which
the Covenant affords. All nations, whether members of the League or not, have pledged themselves
in the Pact of Paris never to use war as an instrument of policy, or for any other purpose than self-
defence.

It might appear that these agreements have
already secured the main end, since all nations
have abandoned their irresponsible sovereignty in

this all-important sphere. But this is not enough. The nations do not trust one another. Moreover, there is a loophole for war under the Covenant of the League. There is a loophole even in the Pact of Paris, since wars of defence are permitted. Consequently all the nations feel that they must be ready for war; their preparations go on just as if neither League nor Pact had ever been adopted; and the sense of insecurity is as great as ever.

If the collective system is to be made a reality, all nations must be enabled to feel (1) that other and better methods than war are available for settling the differences out of which wars arise; and (2) that each of them can securely count upon being protected by overwhelming strength against any aggressive action by another nation in defiance of its undertakings.

The Covenant of the League was intended to meet both of these needs. It provided for an International Court to decide all "justiciable" questions; but some of the nations have been reluctant to pledge themselves to accept the decision of the Court, even on the limited range of cases which its jurisdiction covers. It contemplated a system of arbitration for questions not suitable for judicial decision; but no progress has yet been made towards the establishment of a general system of this kind. It provided that the Council of the League should play the part of a mediator when war seemed imminent, and this function has been successfully performed in a number of instances; but the case of Italy and Greece in 1923, and the case of Japan and China in 1931, have shown that the Council cannot be trusted to act firmly when a Great Power threatens a weak Power. It is clear, therefore, that the methods of securing a peaceful settlement which have hitherto been made available are not such as the nations can be expected to rely upon.

It is equally clear that there is not yet sufficient assurance of protection against aggressive action in defiance of the Covenant. The Covenant provided for combined action against any Power which disregarded its obligations: it contemplated combined economic pressure in the first instance, to be followed possibly by combined military action. But it has been made clear that few nations, if any, are willing to commit themselves beforehand to take action against a recalcitrant Power as the Council may direct. Each nation insists upon deciding for itself, in each case, whether it will take action or not. In these circumstances, the provisions of the Covenant become practically inoperative; they cannot, while they remain mere words on paper, create the sense of security which they were intended to create, or make the nations feel that it is no longer necessary for them to be ready for war.

Accordingly, almost since its foundation, the League has been engaged in trying to discover some form of mutual guarantee which the nations will accept and trust. In 1923 it drew up a general Treaty of Mutual Guarantee, which was promptly rejected by Britain. Next year it produced a much more detailed and highly wrought plan, which was embodied in a Protocol. All the signatory Powers were to accept, and pledge themselves to utilise, an elaborate system of arbitration, and to take combined action against any State which refused to resort to this method of settling differences or to abide by the decision of the arbitrators. This plan, also, was summarily rejected by Britain; and, as unanimity was indispensable, the whole plan fell to the ground.

The reasons for this rejection were in themselves valid; and they usefully illustrate the difficulties of the problem. Broadly, they were two. In the first place, Britain feared that, because of her world-wide interests, such a scheme would involve her in obligations of unpredictable magnitude in every part of the globe—the more so as, in almost every case that was likely to arise, the British fleet would be called upon to play the principal part in any economic blockade. In the second place, the countries which remained outside of the League—notably America—would not be bound by the Protocol; they might offer active opposition to the measures proposed by the League Council; and this would lead to the most dangerous complications.

Two conclusions emerge from this story of failure. The first is that, in the present restless state of the world, no Great Power, with heavy responsibilities, is likely to accept any scheme that will involve it in indefinite liabilities, and possibly in dangerous complications in every part of the world. The second is that no system of collective guarantee can be fully effective so long as powerful States, such as America and Russia, remain outside of its scope.

II. *The Pact of Paris.*

A way out of the second of these difficulties seemed to be offered when in 1928 America invited all the nations of the world to sign the Pact of Paris, whereby they were to pledge themselves never to use war as an instrument of policy, and never to wage any but defensive wars. This action on America's part may be taken as an indication that she was beginning to be uneasy about her aloofness from the international movement and wanted to find some means of forwarding world-peace which would justify her abstention from the League of Nations. Not only was this Pact initiated by America, it was signed by Russia as well as by all other countries; and therefore seemed to provide a new foundation for a system of peace. But the Pact of Paris has proved to be quite ineffectual as a r eans of dispelling fear and creating security; and this for two reasons. It did not—indeed it could not—debar " defensive " war; it left each nation to define for itself whether a war was defensive or aggressive; and as most of the wars of history have been represented as defensive by the countries that waged them, this deprived the Pact of most of its value. Secondly, it included no provision for common action against any nation which should break the Pact; indeed, America made it plain that she had no intention of assuming any such responsibility. It was therefore quite useless as a means of creating among the nations a sense of security.

Since all nations have accepted it, the Pact of

Paris *might* be made the foundation of a system of peace and security; but only on certain conditions. The chief of these is that any breach of the peace between nations should be put on the same footing as a breach of the peace between individuals. If two men begin to fight, it is the duty of the police —and, in the absence of the police, of all good citizens—to *stop the fight*, without inquiring into the rights and wrongs of the question in dispute: these can be determined either by a private agreement or in the law-courts, which exist for that purpose. If the signatories of the Pact agree, they can stop all fighting by immediately putting an end to all diplomatic and commercial relations with any State whose troops cross the frontier of another State, and by making it clear that the territorial or other results of a war will not be recognised by the world. The recalcitrant State—both States, if need be— would thus be outlawed, until they agreed to settle their differences by peaceful means. But this involves two things: first, there must exist some authority which can declare that a breach of the Pact has occurred, and whose decision will at once be accepted by all nations; for prompt action is essential. Will the nations—above all, will America —accept this condition? If so, the required authority must either be the League of Nations or the same thing under another name. The second condition is that some accepted method of peaceful settlement must be available; and as yet no universally accepted method exists, though the International Court (for some purposes) or an *ad hoc* arbitration tribunal (for others) might be used.

An agreement of this sort would have another consequence. All the existing laws of war at sea would go by the board and the age-long dispute about neutral rights and the Freedom of the Seas would come to an end. For a century and a half America has claimed that in time of war all neutral commerce should be free from interruption; while Britain has claimed that the right of interfering with neutral trade when it aids the enemy is essential to the operation of sea-power. Under the system described in the previous paragraph, this long controversy would become meaningless. The Freedom of the Seas for all law-abiding countries could be laid down as an unalterable principle of international law. The distinction between the rights of neutrals and those of belligerents would be otiose; because there would be no neutrals when a particular State was outlawed by the world, and all trading with it would become illegal.

Is there any likelihood that the whole world will accept these principles? If so, the Pact of Paris will genuinely mean the ending of all war, and armaments (for any but police purposes) will become a silly waste of money, in which no country will engage. But if not, the Pact of Paris will be displayed as an empty and futile gesture, without real value except as an expression of sentiment.

There is as yet little sign that America has realised the importance of this dilemma, or that she is willing to contemplate so complete an abandonment of her irresponsible sovereignty in questions of war and peace as the plan described above would involve. Nor does it seem likely that other nations would be ready to go so far, or to trust to the operation of such a system to protect them against danger. They are reluctant to face the risks of war; but they seem to be still more reluctant to face the possible risks of a system of peace. Sooner or later, they must make up their minds which set of risks they prefer.

At the moment America, the most powerful State in the world, seems to be the least awake to the necessities of the situation. But there are signs of a growing readiness on her part to take co-operative action with other States. When Japan took the aggressive against China in 1931–32, a clear case arose under the Pact of Paris; and, as both China and Japan were members of the League, the provisions of the Covenant ought also to have come into effect. China appealed to the League; but no action was taken—probably because the Council of the League is very hesitant about taking any action when a Great Power is involved, and some of its members (notably Britain) feared that they might be involved in dangerous complications in the Far East. They preferred to let it appear that the League was unable and unwilling to take any effective action for the protection of one of its own members; and by adopting this attitude, they struck the heaviest blow at the authority of the League which it has yet endured. America, however, took a stronger line, informing Japan that she would not recognise any changes brought about by a breach of the Pact of Paris. This might have had decisive effect if it had been supported by the other Powers, and especially by Britain. It offered to the members of the League, and especially to Britain, a valuable opportunity of common action with America, hitherto so hesitant about co-operation. But the other Powers, and especially Britain, refused to take the chance.

More recently America has made a further advance beyond the purely negative attitude she has hitherto maintained. Her Secretary of State, Mr. Stimson, and her President, Mr. Hoover, declared in 1932 that America is willing to consult with other signatories of the Pact as to the steps which should be taken when a breach of the Pact occurs. That is a real advance; though it has not yet been endorsed by the Senate, which has the last word on all international agreements to which America is a party, and is apt to take a strongly nationalistic line. This declaration holds out some hope that the Pact of Paris may become more than an empty form of words.

III. *Possible Devices for Security.*

The difficulty of preventing a breach of the peace when preventive action depends upon the will of so many different nations has led some thinkers to fall back upon the plan of equipping the League with an effective force for this specific purpose. The first contribution of France to the Disarmament Conference of 1932 was a plan of this sort under which all the nations were to agree to place certain parts of their forces at the disposal of the League. France saw in this project the promise of a security which might make it possible to reduce national armaments. But nothing came of the proposal; it was suggested that France's main motive was a desire to shelve the direct discussion of disarmament. It has also been suggested that the League should be given control of the latest, the most formidable, and the most mobile and swift in action of all modern implements of war—aircraft. Under this plan, the League alone, by agreement among all the nations, would maintain military aircraft; while civil aviation would be placed under its regulation and control, since civil aircraft can be rapidly turned to military uses. The world's air force, controlled by the League, would be concentrated at a few strategic points, on neutral territory, and would be used solely for the swift stoppage of breaches of the peace. It may be doubted whether, until the authority and impartiality of the League are more firmly established, the nations would be ready for so drastic a step: they might fear that the Commander of so great a force might be tempted to abuse his power—if not in his own interest, then in that of the country to which he belonged. In any case, the mere prevention of breaches of the peace is not enough, unless an accepted method of peaceful settlement is available.

Every argument thus leads to the same conclusion: that the root of the whole matter is the need for a method of settling international differences which the nations will accept and trust. There has been only one experiment of this kind since the war for which success has been claimed—the Locarno agreements; and the outstanding feature of the Locarno system was that the scope of the agreements was limited, and that the guarantors knew the extent of the obligations they were undertaking. At Locarno, Germany on the one hand, and France and Belgium on the other, agreed to settle their differences by arbitration, while Britain and Italy guaranteed the agreements, pledging themselves to join forces against whichever of the parties was false to them. The scheme was brought under the auspices of the League, whose general sanctions were also in reserve to enforce observance. The special merit of this arrangement was that the responsibility of the guarantee was undertaken by specific Powers; it was not made indefinite by being made universal. It is possible that Locarno may be made the model of a series of similar guaranteed agreements between pairs or groups of States in whose case there seem to be exceptional dangers of conflict—each agreement being made in conjunction with a settlement of the outstanding differences between the States concerned. A comparatively small number of guaranteed agreements of this type would cover all the regions in which the clash of war is seriously to be feared. The responsibility for ensuring that the agreements were observed would in each case be undertaken by neighbouring States, but the whole series would be under the ægis of the League, and would be further guaranteed by its general sanctions. This piecemeal and gradual mode of advance may prove to be the most satisfactory way of banishing the fear of war.

In many other cases, where there are no very obvious causes of friction, it should be possible to dispense with specific guarantees; the parties might pledge themselves, in arbitration treaties of the most extensive kind, to refer to arbitration all differences not capable of being decided by the International Court; and the treaties would all be placed under the general guarantee of the League of Nations. It would probably be easier, in the present state of the world, to proceed in this piecemeal manner than to get the assent of all nations to a universal and uniform system of arbitration such as the Protocol defined; but the one might lead to the other. If one or more of the Great Powers—and why should not Britain take the lead?—would set to work to negotiate treaties of " all-in " arbitration with every country willing to conclude them, as the United States did with its Bryan treaties at the beginning of the war, a vast deal might be done towards exorcising that spirit of distrust and fear which is the greatest obstacle to a peaceful world-order.

IV. *Disarmament.*

There remains to be considered the problem of disarmament. Ever since the League of Nations was established, men have argued as to whether security or disarmament comes first. Some urge that the nations will never disarm until they feel secure; others that armaments are the chief cause of insecurity, and that there is no use talking about security until the nations have consented to disarm. The discussion is as unprofitable as the similar argument about the priority of the hen and the egg.

It is certain that there will be no complete or adequate disarmament until the organisation of peace is solid and trustworthy. But, on the other

138

hand, the fear which broods over the world, and is the chief cause of the delay in achieving real peace, springs largely from the nightmare dread of what modern war can do. It is because war has become so hideous, because the ruin and suffering it can bring are so dreadful to the imagination, that all the nations dread the possibility of being caught unprepared, and therefore spend their substance in preparations which only increase the danger. It is sometimes said that the mere horror of modern methods of destruction will be the best preventive of war. But this is only a half-truth. The dread of these horrors makes people fearful and suspicious of one another, forces them to strain their strength to be ready to meet them, and may (as in 1914) tempt them to end the strain by striking when they think they have the advantage. If the nightmare could be allayed, the voice of reason, teaching other ways of getting security, might be heard more readily.

If the world would only recognise the fact, it has already discovered and applied the best means of exorcising this dread; nay, more, it is under an honourable obligation to apply these means on a world-wide scale. The remedy is to prohibit, by agreement, the preparation and use of the weapons which chiefly inspire this dread. One of the main features of the disarmament of Germany was the total prohibition of what were called " weapons of aggression "; and these included battleships of more than 10,000 tons, heavy mobile artillery, military aircraft, tanks, and submarines—the very weapons which are most terrifying. When the allies

gave a formal pledge to Germany that her disarmament would be followed by the disarmament of
other countries, it was surely implied that this
prohibition would be made universal. The provision would be practicable, because, for the most
part, the construction of these weapons cannot be
concealed. If all the nations could agree upon
this action, they would not only deal justly by
Germany and do something to allay her bitter sense
of grievance; they would not only greatly reduce
their own wasteful expenditure (for these weapons
are among the most costly elements in military
outlay); they would strengthen the defensive,
diminish the temptation to attack, exorcise the
nightmare which is the chief cause of the world's
unrest, and make the establishment of a collective
system of peace far easier. And, since they have all
pledged themselves never to use war as an instrument of policy, there is no reason why they should
not take this step, which would be more logical,
simple and just than any plan of proportionate
reduction such as President Hoover proposed.

The greatest disappointment of the first stage in
the Disarmament Conference of 1932 was the fact
that only one of the Great Powers had the courage or
imagination to urge this simple and straightforward
proposal. The others confined themselves to sugges-
tions for the *limitation* of weapons of attack. They
allowed themselves to be befogged and led astray by
the wire-drawn arguments of the technical experts,
who revelled in demonstrations of the difficulty of
drawing the line between weapons of attack and
weapons of defence, asked whether fortress guns

running on rails were mobile or not, and how far the rails must be extended before they became mobile, and argued that big battleships must not be regarded as aggressive weapons. Nobody ever gave to the experts the obvious answer to their conundrums, which is that they had found no technical impossibility in carrying out the prohibition in the case of Germany, and that the rules laid down in her case might quite well be made applicable to all other countries. The prohibition of " weapons of aggression " by general agreement would be only a first step on the road to disarmament; but it would immensely help to create that sense of security which would make the organisation of peace, and therefore further measures of disarmament, possible.

Nor is that the only reason for such a measure. If, twelve years after the conclusion of peace, the nations are not ready to take even this step towards fulfilling the pledge given to Germany, they must recognise that Germany will be morally entitled to rearm, and that, in the present temper of her people, she is very likely to insist upon doing so. That would open a new competition in armaments, which sooner or later, and sooner rather than later, would lead to a new and more terrible conflagration. The world has to choose between boldly taking the necessary steps for the establishment of a collective system of security, and plunging into an abyss from which there may be no recovery. It is not possible to go on dallying indefinitely; for if the wiser choice is not firmly and quickly made, the worse choice will have to be accepted.

A retrospect of the years since the war is full of disappointment for those who hoped that the lessons of the war had been learnt. Nevertheless, something has been achieved, and the nature of the problem has at any rate been made more clear. It may be useful to summarise the conclusions of our analysis.

(1) All nations have, in principle, agreed to abandon their irresponsible sovereignty in regard to war and peace, and to trust to a collective system for their security.

(2) Mere undertakings not to go to war, though useful as an expression of sentiment, are of no value unless there is assurance that any breach of these undertakings will be prevented or punished by the common will; and unless there is an accepted alternative method of settling differences other than war.

(3) An International Court, which commands the respect of the world, has been established and is working successfully. But it can only deal with " justiciable " cases. Other cases can only be dealt with effectively by means of arbitration; but it has not yet been found possible to create a general system of arbitration which all nations can accept and trust, because the obligations implied in it are too indefinite to be willingly accepted by the nations.

(4) A partial and regional arbitration system, under the specific guarantee of two Great Powers, has been set up under the Locarno agreements. This method is capable of being applied to other cases in which there is serious danger of friction; and all-in arbitration treaties without formal

142

guarantees can be made in many other cases. In this piecemeal way, the foundations can be laid for a general system of arbitration.

(5) The Pact of Paris, being (unlike the League of Nations) inclusive of the whole world, can be made the means of preventing breaches of the peace, if all the signatories are prepared at once to outlaw, and sever all relations with, any State which breaks the peace until it refers the subject in dispute to a peaceful mode of settlement.

(6) Full disarmament must follow, and cannot precede, the establishment of a collective system of security. But the universal prohibition of the production or use of " aggressive " weapons, as defined in the Treaty of Versailles, could (if the nations were willing) be adopted to-morrow, and ought to be adopted as part of the pledge given to Germany in 1919. This, by conjuring away the nightmare of horror which the use of these weapons has created, would create an atmosphere favourable to the establishment of a collective system, and therefore, ultimately, to complete disarmament.

The lines of possible future development are therefore clearly marked; and the establishment of a system of collective security, based upon the pooling of the sovereignty of all nations in this sphere, is attainable without any revolutionary change such as the establishment of the World-State.

CHAPTER VI

C. *Organised Economic Co-operation.*

WHEN, at the end of the war, the victor Powers established the League of Nations, they recognised the need for organised international co-operation in the political sphere, especially for the prevention of war; and in doing so (though they were reluctant to admit this in terms) they recognised the necessity for some limitation of the sovereign rights of all States in this sphere. But (except in one field) they did not recognise the need for organised economic co-operation. The Covenant does not contain a single clause conferring upon the League any specific duties or powers to deal with economic questions. It is apparent, therefore, that the world's statesmen had not, in 1919, realised the economic perils which threatened the world, and from which no country could escape by its own action alone. The war had forced them to realise their political interdependence; the economic crisis of the following years was necessary to bring home to them the even more fundamental fact of their economic interdependence.

I. *The International Labour Office.*

The one field in which the necessity of economic co-operation was realised was the organisation of

Labour; and here the realisation was due to the power which had been acquired in all countries, and most notably in Britain, by organised Labour. In each of the peace treaties a long Part (Part XIII in the Treaty of Versailles) was inserted, defining the methods of international co-operation in regard to labour conditions. It is worth while to dwell for a little upon these provisions, not only for their own sake, but also as a model of the way in which it was then thought that international co-operation could best be organised.

The preamble of the Labour clauses contains a valuable analysis of the reasons for and the objects of common action, which deserves quotation:—

" Whereas the League of Nations has for its object the establishment of universal peace, and such a peace can be established only if it is based upon social justice; And whereas conditions of Labour exist involving such injustice, hardships and privation to large numbers of people as to produce unrest so great that the peace and harmony of the world are imperilled; and an improvement of these conditions is urgently required: as, for example, by the regulation of the hours of work, including the establishment of a maximum working day and week, the regulation of the labour supply, the prevention of unemployment, the provision of an adequate living wage, the protection of the worker against sickness, disease and injury arising out of his employment, the protection of children, young persons and women, provision for old age and injury, protection of the interests of workers when employed in countries other than their own, recognition of the principle of freedom of association, the organisation of vocational and technical education, and other measures; Whereas also the failure of any nation to adopt humane conditions of labour is an obstacle in the way of other nations which desire to improve the conditions in their own countries, the High Contracting Parties . . . agree to the following."

This declaration that a steady improvement of the conditions of life for the mass of working-folk ought to be a matter not merely of national but of international concern, and this recognition that progress in this field must be slow and difficult unless it was undertaken by all nations on a co-operative basis, was a conception new to mankind. It was the clearest recognition of economic inter-dependence that the peace settlements contained. But how were these ends to be achieved?

The treaties established a permanent organisation, known as the International Labour Office. Its staff was to provide for the use of all nations ordered statistical information as to the conditions existing in every country, in the hope that the progressive elements in all countries would strive to imitate one another's best achievements. There were to be regular conferences of representatives from all countries, which would discuss the best methods of advance in the light of varying conditions, and would draw up recommendations and draft Conventions on particular points (such as the establishment of an eight-hours day) for submission to the legislatures of the various countries. It might be assumed that the progressive forces in all countries would strive to secure the adoption of these conventions; but no compulsion could be applied. If, however, any country was notably backward, a report on its conditions might be issued, which would have a certain effect. And if any country, after adopting a Convention, should fail to put it in force, various means of bringing it to a sense of its duty were suggested, including the appointment of a Commission of Inquiry (which all nations would be anxious to avoid); and, in the last resort, a recommendation to the other countries which had accepted the Convention, and which would be damaged by being exposed to competition on unfair terms, that they should take defined steps to penalise the offending country.

The International Labour Office has achieved only a very modest degree of success. It has had to operate in a period of distress, when the excuses for refusing to grant improved conditions to workers appeared to be exceptionally plausible. A steady improvement in working conditions is, in fact, only practicable in a period of steady and growing prosperity. If ever the world knows steady progress in wealth again, the effects of the International Labour Office's work will no doubt be felt.

In the meanwhile its chief value is that it has set an example of the way in which, without any invasion of the self-government of individual States, a common direction can be given to the progress of the world. Does this involve any limitation of the " sovereignty " of the various States? It does and it does not. No State is *forced* by a superior

147

Power to adopt any measures which it would not have adopted of its own free will. But pressure is brought to bear upon the will of every State, and stimulus is given to the progressive elements within it, by the organisation of the public opinion of the civilised world; and in so far as any State gives way to this pressure, it recognises and bows to what may be called the " spiritual sovereignty," over all its members, of an interdependent world. The important thing is that the opinion of a progressive world is given the means of expression; and ultimately opinion is the supreme power in human society.

II. *The Economic Work of the League of Nations.*

Despite the fact that no specifically economic functions had been assigned to it, the League of Nations found itself from the first compelled to address itself to the economic problems which were distressing the world.

The greatest success which it attained during its first decade was the financial reorganisation first of Austria and then of Hungary. But for the League's intervention—undertaken at the request of these States themselves—they would have collapsed in complete bankruptcy, and other European States would have been involved in their ruin. The reconstruction was not permanent, or strong enough to stand the strain of the crisis in which the whole world was involved in the years following 1929; because these two little States, with their great capitals designed as the commercial and administrative centres of wide areas from which they were now cut off, had been left in a fundamentally unhealthy situation by the peace settlements, and are never likely to regain economic health until the Chinese walls of tariffs that surround them have been demolished or greatly lowered. Nevertheless, this reconstructive work saved the situation for a time, and usefully illustrated the value of the services that could be rendered by a central organisation able to enlist the co-operation of several nations.

The League developed a powerful economic organisation of its own, staffed by some of the ablest economists of all countries, whose investigations on the problems of the world, undertaken from an international and not a merely national standpoint, might have been of the highest value if the nations had been ready to take advantage of them. But (as we saw in the last chapter) all nations, during this period of stress, insisted upon treating every question in a purely nationalist spirit, and had not begun to realise that the well-being of each depended upon the well-being of all, and that the difficulties of the time could only be solved by international co-operation. All that the League could do was to organise representative Conferences under its auspices, in which the economists, bankers and industrialists of various countries could hear each other's point of view, and learn to regard the problems that bewildered them from an international as well as from a merely national point of view. In each case the economic staff of the League played an indispensable part in drawing up the agenda of the Conferences, and in collecting and arranging the material for their deliberations. The two most important of these Conferences dealt with the two main causes of world disorganisation in the economic sphere.

The Conference of Brussels, in 1920, dealt with the monetary chaos into which Europe had been plunged after the war and gave sound advice to the governments of all nations in regard to the balancing of budgets and the restoration of sound currency. On the whole, the advice of this Conference was followed by most countries in the course of the next few years; it was followed because they had learnt, by hard experience, the terrible dangers of inflation, and had realised that it was only by common action, or, at any rate, by action guided by common deliberation and aiming at the same objective, that economic health could be regained. The consequence of this first and partial step towards co-operation was the improvement in world-trade that marked the years from 1924 to 1929.

The second Conference, held at Geneva in 1927, dealt with the other great cause of distress—the high tariffs by which the trade of the world was being throttled. It, too, gave sound advice to the nations. A large number of experts, many of whom were engaged in their own countries in the framing of tariff schedules, were persuaded for once to look at the question from the point of view of the world as a whole, and not through the blinkers of nationalism; and the result was that they recognised in the incessant increase of tariffs the main obstacle to world-recovery, and urged that a downward revision all round was essential for the restoration of prosperity. But the advice of this Conference, unlike that of the Brussels Conference, was not listened to by the governments of the world. Trade had improved, though its conditions were unsound; they were all wedded to the belief that they could enrich themselves by restricting their trade one with another; and it needed the terrible collapse of 1929–32 to bring to the major part of the world the first dim realisation of the fact that tariffs were bringing the whole world to ruin.

III. *The Crisis and the Need.*

Even the crisis of 1929 and the following years did not bring the nations to their senses: as we saw in Chapter III, they all tried to mend a state of things which was primarily due to restrictions on trade by inventing fresh restrictions on trade. And, at almost the gravest moment of the crisis, Britain, of all countries, abandoned the free-trade system to which she had hitherto clung, and adopted a system of tariffs wider in its range than even that of the United States, though not so high in its levels.

This meant that the only great creditor country which had hitherto been ready to accept goods in payment of the obligations due to it closed that safety-valve, and therefore added seriously to the difficulties of the world. It has been argued that this may serve to bring the world to its senses, and to make all the nations realise the folly of tariffs. That may possibly be the result, but it certainly was not the intention, of Britain's fiscal revolution. The British abandonment of free trade probably destroys the chance (in any case slight) of Britain's again becoming the financial centre of the world, and again playing the part in the management of the world's monetary system which she played before the war; for her unique position in this regard was unquestionably due to the fact that she offered the one great open market to the world. And, since no other country is in a position to succeed her, it follows that some new organisation must be created to regulate the world's new monetary system, whatever form it may take. The change also gravely imperils, and will perhaps destroy, the supremacy in shipping which Britain has long enjoyed owing to the incessant stream of goods into and out of her ports which her free-trade system encouraged. And it may bring to an end the use of bills on London as the chief medium of exchange for international trade. On all these, and other, grounds the British fiscal revolution of 1932 is of great moment not only to Britain herself, but to the whole interdependent world, of which she used to be the pivot. It marks the culmination of the tariff mania which has raged throughout the world since the war.

Its sequel was the meeting of the British Empire Economic Conference, which was held at Ottawa in August 1932. When the British delegates set forth to Ottawa, it was promised that the Conference would give a lead to the world in the reduction of tariffs with a view to the revival of trade. The actual result, however, has been that the Dominions have insisted upon a considerable extension of the British tariffs, and upon the introduction of a quantitative " regulation of imports " in certain cases, with a quota for Dominion imports; and it is stipulated that Britain must not reduce some of these duties without the consent of the Dominions. It appears, also, that a tariff system against foreign countries, with preferences for the rest of the Empire, may be imposed upon the dependent colonies in tropical Africa, the West Indies, and other parts of the world, where practically open markets have hitherto been afforded to all countries; and this cannot but intensify the world's difficulties. The Dominions offer more favourable terms to British goods. But they propose to do this, in part, by imposing still higher tariffs against foreign goods, and therefore further impeding world-trade. And even where an opportunity of " fair competition " is professedly offered to the British trader, it is on the basis of what is called a " compensatory tariff," whereby imports are raised by dues to the same price as the home-produced goods—a principle which, if systematically applied, would put an end to all international trade. In short, far from setting a good example to the world, the Ottawa Conference has created fresh difficulties in the way of any progress towards sanity.

Nor has the attitude of the United States been more promising. When an International Economic Conference was projected for the autumn of 1932, she made it clear that she would only participate if neither war debts nor tariff-rates were to be discussed. It may be, however, that the remarkable presidential election of 1932 may produce a change of attitude.

Nevertheless, despite all these unhappy omens, the fact that an International Economic Conference is to be held, while a Disarmament Conference is actually sitting, and has not yet admitted failure, and (still more) the fact that the European creditors of Germany have been forced to admit that Reparations cannot now be recovered, suggest that some glimmerings of the significance of interdependence are beginning to visit the nations; and that the lessons of adversity have not been wholly wasted. There is still a chance that the nations may learn the folly of allowing their policy to be controlled by an exaggerated and distorted nationalism in time to avert the disaster which sometimes seems to overhang the whole structure of our civilisation.

There are two fields, in particular, in which a clearer sense of the needs of the world as a whole, and a greater readiness to co-operate in making the world's wealth available for the world's peoples, must be attained if there is to be any hope of our enjoying the prosperity that is within our grasp. These are, a clearing of the channels of trade by the reduction or removal of protective tariffs; and the creation of a sound monetary system, not merely for this country or that, but for the world. How far is it reasonable to hope, in the present condition of the world, for any genuine advance towards either of these ends? And by what means can advance best be made? To these thorny questions we must next address ourselves.

IV. *The World's Monetary System.*

The first necessity for the restoration of prosperity, and for its permanent establishment, is the creation of a monetary system of such a kind that there will be no violent fluctuations of general prices, and that the money of each country can always be exchanged for the money of other countries at a steady level. This is only possible if the amount of money in circulation in the world as a whole, and in each country, can always be kept in proportion to the amount of wealth produced. The system, that is to say, must somehow prevent both inflation (which is an increase of money without an equivalent increase of wealth) and deflation (which is a reduction of money without an equivalent reduction of wealth). It must therefore debar governments from issuing money solely for their own immediate advantage, and it must debar dealers in money from increasing the value of their property by unduly restricting the amount of money in circulation. Only if these objects can be secured will justice be done to both debtors and creditors, to both producers and consumers, to both the owners and the users of capital; only so can the wealth which the world produces be fairly distributed among its peoples. This is, of course, not the only condition of fair distribution; but it is an essential condition.

In an ideal world these needs would be met by the creation of a single world-currency, under the guarantee of a single world-authority, which could be trusted to ascertain scientifically the amount of money needed from time to time, and to regulate its issue justly and efficiently. Perhaps the time will come when all the nations will be able to create, and to trust, a common authority for this purpose. But that time has certainly not yet come; the world is not yet ready to trust any single authority so far, nor is our knowledge sufficiently advanced to make such a system workable.

In the absence of a single world-currency, each nation must continue to be responsible for its own money. But all the nations must agree upon a common standard of values, and upon uniform and trustworthy methods of administering this standard, if they are to be able to trade with one another. Before the war, and again between 1925 and 1931, they were all convinced that the Gold Standard met the need, and that if all nations made their chief money-units correspond in value to a fixed weight of gold, the necessary stability, and the necessary interchangeability, would be automatically secured. But recent and painful experience has proved to them that this is not so: prices, instead of being stable, have collapsed to an unprecedented extent since the Gold Standard was re-established; creditors have been enriched at the expense of debtors, and consumers at the expense of producers, to such a degree that the whole economic system of the world has been brought to confusion.

This has caused many people to doubt whether a return to the Gold Standard is either desirable or practicable. And yet this seems to many to be the easiest course, the only course that would provide the world with an automatic regulator of its output of money. Bankers and financiers mostly advocate this course, because they are accustomed to the Gold Standard, and think they know how it works; and because it is a system which has been worked, and therefore (they assume) can again be worked, without any elaborate machinery of central regulation.

Those who oppose a return to the Gold Standard put forward some very cogent arguments. They contend, in the first place, that it is absurd to fix the value of money in relation to one commodity alone, and to make the value of all other commodities go up or down as the value of gold goes down or up. They point out that as trade expands (and in a decently ordered world it is bound to expand very rapidly), the amount of money required to meet its needs must increase. But the amount of gold which the world produces increases very slowly indeed: it has not even kept pace with the sluggish growth of trade in recent years. If our money is to be fixed to gold, and the amount of money issued is to be limited by the amount of gold available (as it must be, under the Gold Standard), there will be a gradually increasing shortage of money, however well the system is managed; and this will not only hamper the development of trade, it will steadily tend to enrich the owners of money at the expense of the owners of goods, and to benefit the *rentier* at the expense of the producer.

It is urged, therefore, that the value of money should be fixed, not in relation to gold or to any other single commodity, but in relation to things-in-general, to all kinds of wealth. This could be done, it is argued, if the authorities that issue money were to take a fixed level of prices (the level of 1929 is commonly suggested) and were to decide that they would use their power first to bring prices back to that level, and then to keep them steady at that level: if prices went down, they would issue more money; if they went up, they would restrict the issue. This is what is called the system of " managed currency." In this way prices, it is urged, could be kept steady; everybody's money would at all times buy the same amount of things-in-general; and both debtor and creditor, both producer and consumer, would get a fair deal. Various devices to secure this end have been proposed. They are too technical to be discussed here. But they all have the same end in view—to use the power of issuing money in such a way as to keep the *average* of prices steady, an end which can never be secured so long as the value of money is fixed by the value of gold. It may be added that, since Britain left the Gold Standard, the British monetary system has been, to a large extent, " managed " on this principle: the object of the Bank of England has been to keep prices steady, and, in spite of many disturbing factors, it has been remarkably successful in doing so.

To these arguments the advocates of the Gold Standard have their answers ready. They admit the advantages of a steady price-level; they admit that, in theory, this could be secured by the means proposed. But they contend that in practice the system of a " managed currency " would offer not only great difficulties but great dangers. It would put very dangerous powers into the hands of the bank, or the government, or whatever authority undertook the duty of managing the currency; whereas the Gold Standard imposes upon them rigid and automatic rules.

Again, it is asked, how is the average price-level to be determined, seeing that the price-levels of all commodities constantly vary not only in relation to gold, but in relation to one another? No satisfactory means has yet been discovered of determining what is the average price-level: you can't average the price of radium with the price of coal; and the " index-numbers " which economists have worked out are only, at the best, rough approximations. Moreover, what is the price-level to be by which the issue of money is to be determined? Is it to be what is called the " world-price " level? That alone would be of any use if the moneys of different countries are to be equated to one another. But what does the world-price mean? And how is it to be ascertained? Or is the chosen price-level to be that of each country? It is the *British* price-level only, and not the world price-level, that the Bank of England has been trying to keep steady. But the price-levels in different countries vary widely, and are especially influenced by their tariffs. The recent policy of the Bank of England, combined with the fall of world-prices, has in effect helped to conceal the effects of tariffs in raising prices. In a tariff-ridden world with managed currencies, the moneys of various countries will necessarily

159

vary in value as against one another because their
price-levels will vary; and one of the greatest
advantages of the Gold Standard—the exchange-
ability of all Gold Standard moneys at a steady
level, which immensely facilitates trade—is likely to
be lost.

To the argument that the world is not producing
enough gold to provide the increase of currency
which is needed for expanding trade, the answer
is given that the use in internal trade of cheques
and other devices for reducing the use of notes and
coins will make it possible to carry on a vastly larger
volume of trade without any large expansion of
currency; and if only the cheque habit could
become as prevalent in other countries as it is in
Britain and America, the existing volume of gold
would probably be sufficient for a long time to
come, provided—a very big proviso—that it was
fairly distributed among all countries in proportion
to their needs. Some people seem to think that
cheques are a sort of false money, and that the
wholesale use of them is a kind of uncontrolled
inflation. But this is nonsense. Money itself is
only a conventional device for facilitating the
exchange of goods for other goods; and cheques
are a device for transferring from A to B the right
to call upon the money which A has in a bank,
thus avoiding the transfer of it from hand to
hand.

But there is another, and a more formidable,
objection to the Gold Standard. It will only work
if the available stock of gold is fairly distributed
over the world; and we have seen three-quarters

of the world's gold concentrated in two countries, where most of it is idle and useless, while all the other countries are left with an insufficient supply, with the consequence that money becomes too scarce, and prices fall disastrously. If the Gold Standard is to be restored in any form, it must be on the basis of an equitable distribution of the available stock of gold. How is this to be brought about? And, if it *is* brought about, how is this equitable distribution to be permanently maintained? It would seem to be impossible either to establish or to maintain such a state of things so long as the nations cling to their high tariffs. For, in a tariff-ridden world, all the creditor countries make it as difficult as possible for their debtors to make payment in goods: even Britain has now adopted this attitude. And the result *must* be, so long as all countries are required under the Gold Standard to sell gold at fixed rates for their money, either that all the gold in the world will gradually accumulate in the creditor countries, and the Gold Standard will be made unworkable; or that the debtor countries will refuse to part with their gold, and the Gold Standard will break down once more. It only worked before the war because Britain, then the great creditor country, was a free-trade country and admitted freely the goods of all countries in payment of their obligations.

It is often said that this difficulty could be overcome if the creditor countries would keep on relending the whole, or the bulk, of what came to them as interest on their loans. But this cannot go on indefinitely. The bigger the debts to the creditor countries become, the greater becomes the difficulty of paying the interest on them; and no country is going to go on for ever supplying more and more capital to other countries with no prospect of ever getting a return. The only way in which it can possibly get a return is by receiving more goods than it sends out; and as soon as a protectionist country discovers that it is doing this, there are shrieks about the " flood of imports " causing an " adverse balance of trade." There seems to be no escape from the conclusion that the Gold Standard cannot work in a tariff-ridden world.

Many plans have been put forward for creating a sound monetary system not tied to gold which will secure the twofold object of stable prices and stable exchanges: some of them are ingenious, others fantastic. There is, indeed, no subject which is more exposed to cranks and panacea-mongers, who put forward their plans as infallible remedies for all the world's troubles. It is often assumed that mis-management of the monetary system is the sole cause of economic chaos, and that the ring of wicked financiers who have control of the issue of money have used their power for their own enrichment, indifferent to the world's sufferings. This is, of course, mere nonsense. The breakdown of the Gold Standard, which worked well enough before the war, has undoubtedly been a very important contributory factor, but it has only been one among many causes of the world's present troubles. It has bewildered the financiers and bankers, who have been accustomed to regard the Gold Standard as a safe anchorage. They long to return to it, because they understand it, and feel themselves at sea when they lose touch with it. They have been reluctant to admit its failure, and all the more reluctant because its premature re-establishment in 1925 undoubtedly favoured the financial interests at the cost of the industrial interests. They feel that the Gold Standard did at least secure stable exchanges between all countries which adopted it; and, as dealers in money, they value stable exchanges more highly than steady price-levels, which the Gold Standard has flagrantly failed to secure. If a choice has to be made between stable exchanges and steady price-levels, the financiers will on the whole give the preference to stable exchanges, while industrialists will give the preference to steady price-levels; and this conflict of interests must be kept in view.

We need not here discuss the various schemes of monetary reform which are being advocated to-day. They must be discussed by experts and decided upon if possible by international agreement, at all events among the principal nations. This is the important thing which here concerns us: there must be a common plan for the management of money, accepted by the nations; and this means that in this vital respect each nation must forgo its irresponsible sovereignty.

What reason is there to hope that, at an early date, all the nations will agree upon a monetary system? France and America, with their great stocks of gold, are likely to insist upon a return to the Gold Standard; and in all countries the financial interests are likely to take the same view. But, as we have seen, this is only possible on two conditions: first that, by some means, a fair distribution of the world's gold stock can be brought about; and secondly that a great reduction of tariffs can be ensured, especially in the creditor countries. If this can be done, it is possible that the Gold Standard may get a new lease of life which may last perhaps for a generation, until a better system has been wrought out. But a restoration of the Gold Standard without a great reduction of tariffs, without a redistribution of gold, and without an agreed international system for securing its fair working, would only lead to a new period of financial chaos.

In any case, it is to be hoped that the nations will be able to agree upon a plan; for the recovery of trade must be retarded if the world is divided between one group of nations which adheres to the Gold Standard, following America and France; and another group which, following Britain, works with a "managed" currency. And it is not enough that they should agree upon a plan. Whatever the system decided upon, somebody must "manage" it; for every monetary system, even the Gold Standard, has to be "managed" in some degree. Before the war, it seemed as if the Gold Standard worked automatically, and many people think that this is still the case; but it worked only because it was informally and almost unconsciously "managed" by the London money-market. There were, as we have seen, two reasons why Britain was able to perform this function. The first was that she was the supreme creditor country of the world; the second that she was the only great free-trade country, and readily took goods, as well as gold, in payment for what was due to her. She has ceased to be the supreme creditor country, and she has also ceased to be a free-trade country; and therefore she cannot regain the financial pre-eminence which she once enjoyed, or become again the pivot of the world's financial system. The United States might possibly succeed to this position; but not while she adheres to high protection. It is, indeed, very unlikely that any single country will ever again occupy the position which Britain occupied in the nineteenth century. Therefore the world must somehow devise for itself a new regulating authority for its monetary system, whether it decides to attempt a return to the Gold Standard or not.

How is this to be done? Can the League of Nations undertake this vitally important function? It can undoubtedly give most valuable guidance, being able to command the co-operation of the ablest monetary experts of all countries, and to inspire them with an international instead of a narrowly national outlook upon the problem. It could, if its members agreed, appoint a standing Commission to watch the development of whatever system may be adopted and to give sound advice to all the nations, just as it is going to appoint a Disarmament Commission. But it can scarcely undertake the business of directly regulating a matter so complex.

There are two recent developments which give ground for hope that the nations may find their way to a workable system of co-operation under common regulation. One is the fact that in recent years almost every country has adopted the same, or nearly the same, rules for the management of its monetary system. They have all taken this function out of the hands of their governments, and entrusted it to Central Banks, constituted by law, with strictly defined powers and not working for a profit. The other is the fact that in 1929, as a consequence of the new settlement of German reparations reached in that year, an international bank, under international control, and known as the Bank of International Settlements, has been set up at Basle, on the neutral territory of Switzerland. Its function, in the first instance, was merely to deal with the reparation payments due from Germany, and as these have now come to an end, its *raison d'être* might seem to have disappeared. But it was anticipated from the outset that it would probably be used for much larger purposes than this. It may well become the Bank of Central Banks, just as each Central Bank is the Bank of Commercial Banks. It may be able to perform for the banking and monetary system of the world something like the functions which the Federal Reserve Board performs for the banking and monetary system of the United States.

The nations have at last realised that they must deal in conclave with the vital question of money. This is to be one of the main subjects of the World Economic Conference, which will probably meet in the spring of 1933. They have to deal with very complicated and highly technical subjects, subjects upon which the layman hesitates to express any confident opinion, subjects which are nevertheless of vital import for the well-being of the world. They have to decide upon what basis the monetary system of the world is in future to be established, and by what organs it is to be managed. If their decisions are to be of any value, they must involve a very important restriction of the sovereignty of all nations in a sphere in which the rights of sovereignty have always been jealously regarded. If they decide wrongly, or if the nations show themselves too jealous of their sovereign rights, they may help to drive our interdependent world nearer to collapse; but if they decide rightly, they will assuredly have done a very great deal to make the world's abundance readily available to the world's peoples.

V. *The Problem of Tariffs.*

It is by international trade that the members of the interdependent world are sustained and are held together. The regulation of the conditions under which this trade is carried on is therefore a matter which concerns them all, and in which they should all have a voice. It cannot be healthy that these conditions should be exclusively determined by each of the nations for itself without regard to the rest.

The open seas, beyond the three-mile limit, forming the larger part of the area of the globe, are not subject, on any interpretation, to the sovereignty of any single State. They ought to be regarded as subject to the sovereignty of the civilised world as a whole. There ought to be a code of laws of the sea, defining the rules which should be observed by all who use these trackless highways, with common laws regarding the safety of travellers, the duties of mutual aid, the rules of salvage, and so forth. There already exists, of course, a large body of well-observed usages, created by the practice of the seafaring peoples during centuries. They should be codified, placed under the ægis of the League of Nations, and enforced mainly by the ordinary courts of all nations, but in some cases by the International Court.

In a growing degree, the control of main routes of transport by sea between various countries is being monopolised by private agreements between powerful shipping concerns of different countries, which are tempted sometimes to abuse their power. No single State can adequately control these combines, yet they need to be controlled, and it should be the business of some international authority to define the conditions within which they should work and to provide remedies against abuses. This is no easy problem to solve. But it must be solved; and it can only be solved by international co-operation.

In the same way, huge combines and working agreements are establishing monopoly conditions in various types of production, which disregard frontiers. It is part of the duty of every State to guard its citizens against the possible evil consequences of monopoly. But in these cases, no single State can possibly exercise effective control without the aid of international co-operation. There is already international co-operation among the *organisers* of monopoly; it is equally needed for the *regulation* of monopoly, and for the definition of the rules which every State should apply within its own limits.

Some of these great combines are also beginning,

by private agreements, to try to define the world's requirements of this commodity or that, and to apportion among various countries the supply of this demand. It may be that some sort of rationing, after this manner, is needed; but it has very obvious dangers, and, if it is to be done at all, it ought to be done under the supervision of some body representing the interests of all the nations. Perhaps, as the interdependence of the nations increases and the impossibility of effective and just regulation by isolated States becomes more obvious, something like the Inter-State Commerce Commission of the United States will be found to be necessary for the world as a whole. It will obviously involve some practical limitation of the irresponsible sovereignty of the nations in these spheres; but it may prove to be the best means of preserving their real freedom, just as the regulation of monopolies by the State is the best means of preserving the freedom of individuals.

The development of co-operative regulation in the sphere of trade which we have touched on in the foregoing paragraphs relates to needs of the future, perhaps of the near future, which have not yet become very urgent. But there is one form of trade-regulation, the most drastic and the most dangerous of all, which has been carried to such a pitch by the irresponsible sovereignty of the nations that it threatens ruin to the whole world, unless some immediate co-operative action can be taken to diminish its extravagances, and to bring about a return to sanity. This form of regulation is Tariffs, whereby all States strive to force international trade to flow in channels of their own devising, with the consequence that they have almost brought it to a standstill.

The tariff problem is, indeed, the greatest and the most fundamental of the world's economic problems. Tariffs are, beyond question, the chief cause of the world's sufferings. They are the indirect cause of the monetary dislocation which we discussed in the last section, and unless they are firmly dealt with, they are likely (as we have seen) to make it almost impossible to construct an efficient monetary system for the interdependent world. They have turned international trade from a mode of mutual aid into a mode of warfare, from a unifying to a disuniting force. They are the chief obstacle in the way of a wide diffusion of prosperity, because they prevent the flow of the world's abundance to the impoverished peoples of the world. Next to war itself, they are the most destructive expression of fevered nationalism. They are the means whereby the nations pursue the vicious and unattainable aim of self-sufficiency, and thereby prevent interdependence from yielding the rich fruits it can give to humanity. They are the most mischievous outcome of irresponsible sovereignty.

What chance is there that, at this critical moment in the world's history, the nations will recognise where the root of their troubles lies and deal with it in agreement? At the moment, it would appear, very little chance indeed. For although, when they gather round the conference table, as they did at Geneva in 1927, they will all agree that tariffs are ruining the world, each of them interprets this to mean that it is the tariffs of the other nations that are to blame: each nation's own tariffs are merely necessary measures of self-defence. And they return from passing these pious resolutions to create fresh tariffs of their own and to invent other methods of restricting trade. Thus the British delegates went to Ottawa declaring that an example must be given to the world of the need for reducing tariffs; and they came away from Ottawa pledged to impose a whole series of new tariffs, together with " quantitative regulation of imports " and quotas—pledged also not to reduce many of these restrictions without the consent of the Dominions!

All the nations seem to be bemused by two ideas: the first, the idea that it is undesirable to buy from abroad anything that can be produced at home; the second, the idea that it is essential (in so far as any international trade is carried on) that each nation should have a " favourable balance of trade " and sell more than it buys. These two superstitions are ruining the world.

The first of these superstitions leads governments, by means of tariffs, to encourage the production of goods which their country cannot produce as well as other countries. In doing so they deprive their own people of free access to the world's abundance; they impoverish them by making them pay higher prices for what they buy, and therefore leave them with less power to purchase other goods; and they add to the cost of producing the goods which the country is best fitted to produce, and therefore make it more difficult to sell these goods in other countries. It is possible to grow bananas in Lancashire (under glass, with artificial fertilisers and artificial heat and sunshine) instead of importing them from the Canaries; but they would cost so much that few would be able to afford them, unless everybody was taxed to pay for the necessary equipment; and it is surely better to produce cotton goods in Lancashire and exchange them for bananas growing in the Canaries. It is possible to grow sugar in Lincolnshire; but this competition with the tropical sun can only be carried on at vast expense to the taxpayer, and it is surely better that Lincolnshire should not be crippled by fresh taxes in producing agricultural machinery that can be exchanged for the sugar of Demerara. The only possible justification for trying to produce at home goods that can be got better and cheaper abroad is the fear that a country may be cut off from the foreign supplies or be unable to pay for them. But the country that suffers from either of these things, in an interdependent world, is in any case doomed to ruin: if it cannot pay for goods from abroad, it certainly cannot pay for producing them more expensively at home.

The superstition about the necessity of a favourable balance of trade is even more foolish. It is easy to see why a nation might want to buy (on credit) more than it sells: this may be the best way of developing its own resources, and it will not long get credit unless it is going to use it in that profitable way. But why should it want to sell more than it buys? Is it because it will get more *money* that way? But money has no value except for the purchase of goods or services in the country which issues it. If German goods are sold in Sweden, they will be paid for in Swedish money, which has no value outside of

Sweden, and can only be used to buy Swedish goods or services; if not so used, it will have to be left in Sweden as an investment. No country, therefore, can gain *money* as the result of a " favourable balance." It may gain gold, to a limited extent, if the countries with which it trades are willing to part with their gold; and up to a point, but not beyond it, this may be beneficial. It may gain wealth in the form of goods, though this will be the increase of imports which all countries are trying to check. But it cannot increase its stock of useful money except by issuing more itself, which it can only safely do if it has increased its earnings. The notion that the object of foreign trade is to increase a country's money, or even its gold, is a hoary fallacy which, under the name of Mercantilism, was shown up long ago by all the standard economists. The object of foreign trade is to obtain goods which the country cannot so well or so cheaply produce itself; and the fewer of its own goods a country has to export in order to pay for these imported goods, the more it will profit. It is for the sake of imports that trade is carried on; and exports are only valuable as a means of paying for imports.

Nobody in America troubles his head about the balance of trade in Kansas; nobody in Germany about the balance of trade in Mecklenburg; nobody in England about the balance of trade in the Isle of Wight. But why not, if a " favourable balance " is of such vital importance? The Isle of Wight must have a terrific adverse balance, since it exports very little and imports nearly all its requirements. Would it be more prosperous if a tariff was put on all goods coming from Hampshire and Sussex, that is to say, if all its inhabitants were made to pay more for these goods? If the Isle of Wight is passing through a period of distress, nobody suggests that the County Council can mend matters by taxing goods because they come from London or Portsmouth. Everybody recognises that its distress is only a part of the distress of England, the economic entity of which it forms a part; and that it cannot hope to mend matters by disorganising the trade of the greater entity, but only by making the most of its own resources, and so playing its part in the greater entity more efficiently. What is true of the Isle of Wight in relation to England is equally true of the relation of each country to the supreme entity of the interdependent world. The distress of each country is due to the distress of the world as a whole; and no country can better its condition by adding to the disorganisation of the interdependent world, but only by helping to make the currents of world-trade flow more freely.

But it is useless to labour an argument which every nation recognises to be sound for all other nations, but not for itself. Each might confess: *Video meliora proboque, deteriora sequor*. They will probably meet in conference and pass pious resolutions; but they will go on as before, or perhaps (as in the case of Ottawa) make things a little worse.

The ultimately desirable thing—and probably the ultimately inevitable thing—is that all tariffs should be swept away throughout the world, except for purely revenue purposes; which would mean that (except in the case of goods not produced in the country) every customs duty would be balanced by an equivalent excise duty on the home product. This was the system under which Britain attained to her greatest prosperity and became the pivot of the world's economic order. It would make all the products of the world accessible to all the peoples of the world. It would automatically ensure that the world's productive activities should be carried on in the areas most fitted for them. It is the only system that is in accord with the state of interdependence into which the world has grown; the only system which would allow the process of knitting together the peoples of the earth to go on unimpeded; the only system which treats trade as the conferment of mutual benefits, and not as a form of war; and it would lead to such an immense expansion of trade that the interruption of these processes by war would become not only intolerable but unthinkable.

But it is quite unimaginable that the nations should at once agree to throw down all their tariff walls Even if their prejudices were not too great to make this possible, it would be impracticable, because it would involve an immense disloca-tion of the activities that have grown up under the shelter of tariffs. Every country has used the argument that tariffs are necessary to help the establishment of " infant industries "; but the infants reared in this artificial way seem to suffer from a strange weakness, for no instance has ever been known in which they have become strong enough to walk without their accustomed crutches.

How then will it be possible to get rid of the

barbed-wire fences which, as in the derelict areas of war-time, cumber all the roads of traffic? It seems to be expected that this will be achieved by a process of bargaining between nation and nation; and it has long been one of the favourite theories of tariff-mongers that tariffs are invaluable as " bargaining weapons." Unhappily long experience shows that when the bargaining is undertaken its usual outcome is an increase of tariffs on both sides. Reductions become impossible, because the trades in which the reduction is proposed protest vehemently against being deprived of their protection for the advantage of other trades. If it is hoped that, when all the nations meet in conference, all recognising that the world's distress is due to tariffs, they will all be ready to make equivalent reductions, it ought perhaps to be remembered that all the nations also agree that armaments must be reduced, but do not find it easy in conference to agree upon specific reductions.

The Ottawa Conference is of evil omen for any future conference of the same kind, for its outcome was that Britain was forced to raise her tariffs and to pledge herself not to reduce some of them without the consent of the Dominions. Britain, therefore, who might have been expected to take the lead in negotiations for tariff reductions, and whose leaders have long been declaring that she was imposing tariffs largely in order that she might take them off again as part of a bargain, goes into any conference on this subject with her hands tied. Whatever terms may be proposed to her, she is not permitted to reduce some of her duties; she cannot conclude

176

with any foreign country an agreement for mutual freedom of trade; her Parliament, for the first time in its history, has been deprived of the right to revise its own rates of taxation. In these circumstances it would be foolish to build any high expectations on the outcome of a new economic conference —especially since the United States, whose participation is indispensable, has stipulated that, if she takes part in such a conference, tariff rates must be excluded from the agenda.

Is any method left whereby an attempt may be made to get at the root-problem of the world's distress, the chief factor which makes the economic interdependence of the world a source of danger rather than of benefit? One fact of good augury, and one alone, has recently been made known to the world. Two small nations—both low-tariff countries—Belgium and Holland, have made an agreement for the progressive reduction of their duties against one another's goods; and they have invited any and every nation that cares to do so to join them and share in the advantages of the agreement. This suggests the possibility of what might be called a Free-Trade and Low-Tariff Club of Nations. Each nation joining the Club might agree that (possibly after an interval for adjustment) it would levy no duty higher than (say) 10 per cent. upon the goods of the other members; but it would be free to levy whatever duties it thought fit upon goods from non-member countries. There would be nothing in this arrangement to prevent any member of the Club from abolishing all its duties, or from offering a free market to the other members and levying duties of (say) 10 per cent. on goods from other countries.

Such an arrangement, offering as it would an enlarged market to all its members, might prove to be attractive to many nations, especially if one or more of the greater trading nations were to join in it. Britain, for example, might have been the nucleus of such a Club, and it is probable that her participation would have attracted many nations, because her home market, and the markets of her dependent empire, are among the most desirable in the world. But she has debarred herself from any such action, at any rate so long as the present nationalist regime controls her policy. She has put herself under an obligation to levy duties on the goods sent to her from (for example) Denmark, which gives practically free admission to British goods, in order to give an advantage to (for example) Australia, which places as great impediments in the way of British trade as any other country; and she has also pledged herself to levy duties on goods from foreign countries imported into her dependent empire in order to give advantages to the Dominions and to herself. It is therefore difficult, if not impossible, for Britain to enter into any such agreement as we have described for freer trade; and it is probable that the shackles with which she bound herself at Ottawa will prove to be a very grave obstacle in the way of any general agreement, and perhaps a very serious source of embitterment among the nations.

The tariff problem is the most important and the most urgent of all the problems raised by the threatened wreck of the interdependent world; and of them all, it seems to be the one for which, at the moment when these lines are written, there is least hope of reaching any tolerable solution, unless all the nations, or a large group of them, undergo an unexpected change of heart.

CHAPTER VII

THE IMPERFECTIONS OF THE INSTRUMENTS OF GOVERNMENT

IT is easy to see, and to demonstrate, that all the peoples of the world have become, during the last two generations, unalterably interdependent, and that no one of them can henceforth hope to attain either security or prosperity by its own efforts. It is easy to see, and to demonstrate, that this state of things necessitates a high degree of organised co-operation among the peoples of the world, lacking which their mutual dependence may bring to them not well-being but ruin. It is not difficult to see what are the main functions which must either be performed in common or regulated by common agreements, and even to indicate in outline what ought to be done in regard to each of them. But it is much more difficult to see how this needful co-operation is to be made effective among nations which are all acutely jealous of their independent sovereignty. Is the governmental machinery of the world capable of bringing about the readjustments that must be made if the peoples of the earth are to enjoy the peace and prosperity that are within their reach? No discussion of the theme of this little book would be adequate without some attempt to deal with that question.

I

The response of most people to the question we have just posed would be that the League of Nations has been set up for this precise purpose: if it cannot do what has to be done, it is useless and had better be discarded. That is especially the cry of those who disbelieve in the whole international movement and have not yet learnt the necessity for organised co-operation among the nations. But it is based upon a complete misconception. The League of Nations is not a body independent of, outside of, and above the nations which constitute it. It is merely the machinery through which they can co-operate, if they are willing to do so. It can do nothing unless all its members agree. Even if they agree, each of them must be left to put the agreement into operation for itself. The machinery of co-operation is not to be blamed if those for whom it was designed fail to make use of it.

In any case, the League is an imperfect instrument for its purpose so long as two of the most powerful nations in the world, the United States and Russia, stand aloof from it. One of the most hopeful features of recent years has been the growing readiness of both Russia and the United States to co-operate in its work in various ways, and to take part in the conferences which it summons. They do so because they, like all the other nations of the world, are being forced by the pressure of events to recognise the absolute necessity of some organisation for common purposes. Even though the League has, as yet, realised few of the hopes that its foundation inspired, the sense of the utter need for some such focus for common action is spreading and deepening throughout the world.

It is an essential feature of the system of the League that on all important matters there must be unanimity among its members. No decision can be imposed upon reluctant nations by a majority vote. This may seem almost to foredoom the League to impotence. Yet it is fundamental to its constitution; on no other terms will the nations, in their present temper, consent to co-operate; and it is useless to advocate the introduction of a majority system— there would be no means of enforcing the majority's decision.

As a consequence, the League has to proceed by way of conferences, and by the slow creation of international opinion. It has standing commissions of experts on various subjects, whose reports and recommendations have influence upon the policy of the various governments. It organises special conferences on particular subjects of experts who are nominated by the various governments, but without power to commit them; the economic conferences of Brussels in 1920 and of Geneva in 1927 are examples of this—the first materially influenced the policy of most of the nations, as we have already seen; the second seems to have had no effective influence. Finally, for dealing with great and critical issues, it can organise conferences in which all the governments are represented as governments, while the officials of the League do everything they can to help by preparing material for discussion.

Two great conferences of this kind—the most important in the League's history—have been made necessary by the acute stage of crisis into which the world has passed since 1929. The first is the Disarmament Conference, which met in February 1932, and in which, after twelve years of discussion and preparation, the nations are being challenged to decide whether they are going to fulfil the pledges given in 1919, and to make peace not merely secure, but possible; or whether they are going to drift on towards another and perhaps final catastrophe. The second is the World Economic Conference, which will probably meet in the spring of 1933; and in which the nations will be called upon to decide whether they intend to recognise and act upon their mutual economic dependence, and by doing so ensure prosperity to all; or whether they are going to continue to strive after an un-attainable self-sufficiency, in which each, seeking to enrich itself at the expense of the rest, will contribute to ruin both itself and the rest. No more momentous discussions have ever taken place in the course of human history. They may determine the world's future. The League of Nations has made them possible. It can do no more. The decision must rest with the nations themselves and with their governments.

The method of Conference, by which alone the League can proceed, is undeniably cumbrous and slow; and as these discussions drag out their weary length and agreement is retarded by the fears, jealousy and *amour propre* of this nation or that, eager idealists who see what is needed and cannot under-stand why everybody else does not also see it are very apt to lose patience. And, indeed, it is more than possible that the delays and exasperations of these debates may be so long drawn out that the problems they are meant to solve may become insoluble while they proceed. Yet it must not be forgotten that in these tedious debates the peoples of the earth are, for the first time in their history, striving to find solutions for difficulties which affect them all, but with which they have always been accustomed to deal in isolation, never thinking of the interests of the world as a whole, but only of their own narrower interests. And although experience has shown that this old method will no longer serve the needs of an interdependent world, it is not surprising that the nations and their governments are slow to adjust themselves to these new conditions; and it is something gained that the League and its machinery are there to serve as a constant reminder that the well-being of each is now ineluctably dependent upon the well-being of all.

The League, then, cannot decide these issues itself; it can only provide the nations with the machinery for deciding them; and if this machinery is cumbrous and slow in its working, that is because the nations insist that it must be so. Ultimately, therefore, the question which we posed at the beginning of this chapter—the question whether the governmental machinery of the world is capable of the necessary adjustments—can only be answered by inquiring whether the governmental systems of the various nations are of such a kind as to assist or to hinder the great advances upon which the future of humanity depends.

II

With two notable exceptions, Italy and Russia, all the greater nations of the world are now (at any rate in name and form) governed by democracy. The all but universal adoption of the democratic and parliamentary system took place during the last eighty years—the same period in which the interdependence of the world was being established; and in many cases the system has not yet had time to take root. This ought not to be forgotten; because democracy—the most difficult of all forms of government—can only work well among homogeneous peoples, habituated by long practice to mutual tolerance and an instinctive obedience to law.

At first sight the almost universal existence of democratic systems must appear to be favourable to the establishment of a regime of peace and international co-operation. The mass of the people everywhere want peace, and want prosperity, though they may be vague as to the best means of securing them; and they do not trouble themselves about technical questions of sovereignty. This ought to make agreement between the nations easy.

But, on the other hand, the mass of ordinary people, having little knowledge of other countries than their own, are easily stirred to scorn, fear or anger against other peoples: the sentiment of the navvies, in *Punch's* old drawing—" There goes a bleedin' furriner : 'eave 'arf a brick at 'im "—is by no means dead in any country. And since the competition of parties for power is a feature of all democracies, and party managers will often stoop

185

(secretly if not openly) to any method of arousing prejudice against their opponents, democratic governments are very chary of taking any action which may expose them to the charge of being unpatriotic and of sacrificing the interests of their country. In the interdependent world, the *supposed* interests of a country will often have to be sacrificed for the sake of its *real* interests; but democratic governments, always excessively nervous about possible misrepresentation, are apt to be chary about making the necessary " sacrifices." They know that (for example) the cessation of wasteful expenditure on armaments will always be represented by some not as a gain but as a sacrifice. It is but rarely that democracy throws up statesmen who have the courage boldly to take the right course, and boldly to defend it to their people, at the risk of temporary unpopularity. For it must be recognised that democracy, as it now works, has not in any country served the purpose which it was expected to serve, of sifting out the leaders who deserve leadership by foresight, imagination and courage; but has mainly installed in places of authority men of second-rate quality who seldom look ahead further than the next general election, and whose chief characteristic is timidity.

A hundred years ago, when Europe was for the most part governed by autocracies, and even Britain was under the control of a very limited aristocracy, it was possible for the governments of the Great Powers to announce that they had inaugurated " an era of permanent peace "; and although the foundations of their system were unsound, the agreements on which it was based were swiftly and easily reached, because none of them was inhibited by the fear of criticism by its political opponents. In our own day, Italy and Russia, the two great non-democratic countries, have been able to make far bolder pronouncements on disarmament than any of the democratic governments have dared to make. There is, in truth, no denying that the democratic system is ill adapted for the conclusion of rapid and stable international agreements.

It has also a further defect, which has been acutely felt in recent years. The democratic system necessitates frequent general elections, which may lead to sudden changes in the personnel and policy of their governments. The prospect of an election in any country inevitably introduces an element of uncertainty in the negotiations between it and other countries, which may last for some months and make the process of negotiation seem unreal. There is no country in which the uncertainties thus created are greater, or last longer, than the United States. No conclusive agreements can be reached during the year before a Presidential election, which takes place in November, once every four years. Even when the election is over, the new President does not take office until the following March; and this causes a further prolongation of uncertainty whenever a new President representing a different party and policy from those of his predecessor has been elected. During the critical year 1932, when prompt and vigorous international action was more urgently needed than ever before, there were general elections in both France and Germany, the effect of which was to postpone the discussion of the reparation problem to the eleventh month of the year of grace which had been allowed by the *moratorium* of 1931; there was also a Presidential election in America, which caused the vital World Economic Conference to be postponed for many critical months.

There is no possible means of overcoming this inherent defect of the democratic system for international agreements. The suggestion that general elections should be held at the same time in all countries is merely idle. In one way only could this drawback be minimised. If elections could be conducted in such a way as to reflect the permanent and stable elements in the outlook of the various countries, and not in such a way as to emphasise and exaggerate the " swing of the pendulum," or to give undue weight to the more changeable and mobile elements in the electorate, it would be possible both for individual countries and for the world as a whole to follow a more consistent and steady line of policy. But such a method of election is not likely to recommend itself to the managers of organised parties. They do not desire a stability which will rest upon a fair balance of varying opinions; they want a system which will offer to them the chance of winning an overwhelming domination, such as a genuinely representative system will never yield to any single party.

It therefore appears that the bad working of the democratic system may have the effect of impeding, perhaps even of preventing, the agreements between nations which are necessary for the safety and for the continued progress of our civilisation. At the same time, the defects of the democratic system are manifestly making it difficult for individual nations to carry out the social and economic readjustments that are necessitated by changing conditions; and the conflicts of parties, which are an inevitable concomitant of democracy, are apt, under serious stress, to become so bitter as to threaten the very foundations of order in some countries.

It is for these reasons that in all countries there is discontent with the working of democracy, at any rate in the parliamentary form; while in some it has already been dethroned, temporarily or permanently. In Italy parliamentary democracy has been displaced by a form of Cæsarism—the rule of one man, resting on popular support, but buttressed by armed might and defended by the forcible suppression of free criticism. In Russia it has been displaced by the supremacy of a highly organised and fanatical minority, equally supported by arms and by the forcible repression of criticism. In Germany the authority of the representative body is being over-ridden by the authority of the President, which rests, equally with that of the Reichstag, upon a direct popular vote. Because the Reichstag is reduced to impotence by its party divisions, the authority of the President is upholding a ministry to which the Reichstag would give no support, and Presidential edicts are for the time being taking the place of parliamentary enactments. If the democratic governments of other countries continue to display the wavering timidity which has hitherto marked their attitude towards the most critical problems of modern times, there is no knowing how far this revulsion against democracy may not go.

It is therefore important to form a clear view as to the reasons for the bad working of the democratic system; to inquire whether, or how far, these defects are inherent in democracy, and whether, or how far, they are due to the imperfection of its instruments; and to consider if there are any practical remedies whereby these defects could be either removed or greatly reduced, especially in the conduct of international relations.

III

Most of the defects of the democratic system arise from two causes: from the inattention of the mass of electors, and from the rigidity of party organisation.

The average man and woman, engrossed in the cares of livelihood and in the distractions of the cinema, football and betting, are apt to take very lightly their responsibilities as citizens. For the most part they awaken to a spasmodic interest in politics only during the excitement of an election contest. They know little about the issues upon which they nominally have to decide, and the popular press does little to enlighten them. But they know that each vote is only one among many millions, and—at any rate in the British system—that it does not count for anything at all unless it is cast for a successful candidate: at least two-thirds of the electors of Britain know that they have had no direct share in returning any member of Parliament, and this seriously militates against popular interest in politics.

To study political problems, and to form an independent judgment upon them, may well seem a mere waste of time, seeing that the man who tries to think for himself will probably have no chance of voting for anyone who can express his ideas; for, in effect, all that the democratic elector is allowed to do is to make his choice between candidates who are pledged to suppress their own opinions and to vote for a party. Under the continental system of Proportional Representation the elector does not even vote for an identifiable candidate: he votes nakedly for a party. Under the British system he votes, indeed, for an individual, but the individual is merely the spokesman of a party machine, and, often enough, is manifestly unfit to play a part in the government of a great country—is fit, indeed, only for the part he is going to play, of a voting machine controlled by a party caucus.

It is not surprising that the democratic system, thus worked, does not succeed in creating a sense of civic responsibility; nor is it surprising that, when interest is suddenly awakened by the excitement of an election, the democratic electorate is peculiarly liable to be swung this way or that by panics, stunts or reckless promises. In effect, the deciding voice in every election belongs, not to those who have tried to understand the issues involved, but to a wavering and uninstructed crowd influenced by all sorts of irrelevant and extraneous considerations. Party organisations, striving for power, are, of course, aware of this state of things and utilise it: the temptation to appeal to any prejudice which will damage their rivals is very strong. These dangers are at their greatest in a system such as that of Britain, where the transfer of a few votes in a relatively small number of constituencies may bring about a sweeping change in the composition of Parliament and in the policy of the country, though no great change may have taken place in the balance of public opinion. The instability which arises from this state of things, and the temptation which it offers to politicians to shape their policy so as to please, not the majority, but the margin of unthinking waverers, is a danger even in domestic politics ; but when (as in the interdependent world of to-day) the fate of humanity may depend upon the action of a particular country at a critical moment, the conferment of controlling power upon the least instructed and most variable elements in the community constitutes a real danger.

The incessant conflict of organised parties for power, and the discipline which they strive to impose upon their members, thus tends to vitiate the process of election by turning what ought to be a national debate on many-sided problems into a mere fight for power between rival caucuses and by limiting far too narrowly the choice before the electors. But it has even more serious consequences than these. In effect it excludes from public life many men who could make valuable contributions, because, in order to get an opportunity of public service, they must pledge themselves to vote obediently for a party which is able to assure them of a majority at a particular time and in a particular place. It would be easy to make a list of fifty men in Britain, for example, who are of such outstanding capacity that they ought to be included in any representative national body. These men would obtain the votes of millions if a poll of the whole country could be taken, while the ordinary party member could on such a poll count upon no more than a few thousands of votes; but because they will not toe the party line, or because they cannot obtain a majority at a particular time and in a particular place, the nation must do without the leadership they could give. Party machines are always distrustful of men of independent minds; and the poverty of leadership from which we are suffering in this generation is largely due to this.

Again, it is mainly the working of party discipline that has reduced Parliament to impotence, made it a mere registering machine for the decrees of the party caucus that has been able to snatch an unreal majority at the polls, and undermined the confidence of the people in the parliamentary system. Time was when Parliament did, in fact as well as in theory, really control the process of government. It no longer does so; because it has become the slave of the Cabinet for the time being, and of the party caucus that works through the Cabinet. This, at any rate, is the case whenever a single party has a clear majority. And yet nothing is more certain than that no single party ever, in any country, commands a clear majority of pledged supporters in the electoral body; at the most a party may, in special circumstances, obtain a majority from voters who merely think it less bad than another alternative.

Wherever, on the other hand (as in most continental countries), there are several parties, no one of which obtains a clear majority, the controlling authority of Parliament becomes real; the government is unable to pursue a purely partisan policy, but has to pursue the greatest common measure of national agreement; and national policy, instead of oscillating violently, tends to follow a steady course. In such circumstances governments may change frequently, as in France, or they may hold office for long spells, as in the Scandinavian countries; but in either case the broad continuity of national policy is in normal conditions maintained by the balance of forces in the representative body. It is sometimes said that France suffers from its very frequent changes of ministry, which are due to the multiplicity of its parties; but there is no country which has, on the whole, pursued so coherent and consecutive a policy since the war.

There is still another danger which attends the working of organised parties in the democratic system. Whether parties, in any country, are many or few, they always need money for propaganda and the expenses of elections. This opens an opportunity for organised interests to secure indirect political power; they make contributions to party funds, not because of their disinterested zeal for a cause, but because they expect something in return— tariff protection, or backing for a loan, or (as in the case of the British Trade Unions, which finance and control the Labour Party) the pursuit of a dictated policy. Party funds are the plague-spot of democratic politics: through them " money talks," and too often has the last word. If, for example, a country is ruled by a party which has received large subscriptions from great armament firms, what is likely to be its attitude on disarmament?

The defects of the democratic system which we

have described are obviously more patent in some countries than in others, partly because the machinery is better in some countries than in others, partly because some countries have a better political tradition than others and a steadier and more intelligent electorate. But they are everywhere too plain; they are everywhere perilous, especially because of the obstacles they offer to the effective co-operation of governments which is indispensable in our now interdependent world. And it becomes important to consider whether there are any practicable means whereby, without interfering with the fundamentals of democracy or displacing it by Cæsarism or Sovietism, these defects could either be removed or materially qualified.

First of all, can anything be done to obviate the dangers that arise from the existence of an indifferent, uninstructed and irresponsible electorate, and from the controlling power which falls to the most variable and irresponsible elements in it?

Without affecting the right of every adult to exercise the franchise, it might reasonably be provided that this right should not legally be operative unless and until the voter had made a formal claim, in person or in writing, to be placed upon the register of electors, and this not during the excitement immediately preceding an election, but in normal and quiet times. This would put an end to the *automatic* enrolment of voters, which (in Britain) dates only from 1928: it would imply that the right of voting, while open to all, would only be exercised by those who took their civic rights seriously enough to take a very modest amount of trouble to secure

195

them. It might even be provided that a very small registration fee, of, say, sixpence or one shilling, should be paid by every applicant for this privilege. Once on the register, the voter's name would remain on it without the need for further application, unless or until some special reason appeared for striking it off, such as death, certified lunacy, or the commission of a crime. Failure to vote at any election might automatically involve omission from the register, unless a valid excuse were given in writing; in this case a formal application for readmission would be necessary. The voter might be required to notify the registration officer if he removed to another constituency, and it would then become the officer's duty to notify his colleague in the new constituency so that the voter's name might be at once inserted upon his register; failing which the voter's name would not appear on either register, and a new application would have to be made. The slight amount of trouble which would thus have to be taken to secure civic rights would be in itself wholly reasonable; but it would probably have the effect both of making registers more accurate and of securing the omission of large numbers of people who are totally indifferent to politics except during the excitement of an election. The self-disfranchisement of such voters 'would be a very great gain; a substantial proportion of the unthinking and irresponsible voters who now decide elections would disappear.

This device, sound so far as it goes, would be by no means sufficient to turn elections into a real consultation of the nation, such as they ought to be if democracy is not to be a sham, the plaything of organised interests. Both for the purpose of giving reality to the franchise and for the purpose of making possible the election of men of ability, character and independence, capable of exercising leadership, five things seem to be indispensable. In the first place, every vote cast should count in determining the composition of the representative body; every voter should be able to feel that he was represented by somebody whom his vote had helped to return. In the second place, every substantial body of opinion in the country should be represented in proportion to its strength. This does not mean that there should be so many vegetarians and so many spiritualists, though if there were a sufficient number of people who thought that vegetarianism was more important for the nation's welfare than anything else, they ought to be represented; it means that all the main schools of political thought should have their due weight, and not be left to feel that they were prevented by a vicious system from making their contribution to the national discussion. In the third place, no elector should be limited to a choice between two or three men, no one of whom may seem to him to be a suitable representative of his opinions, or even (as now happens in uncontested seats) be deprived of any right of choice at all; nor should he be compelled to choose between two party programmes, both of which may be in his view wholly unsound. The limitation of the range of choice is one of the greatest defects of the system of single-member constituencies. In the fourth place it should be possible for men of outstanding personality, unwilling to submit themselves to the rigid discipline of a party, to win a secure place in Parliament; and it should be impossible for whole groups of leading men to be suddenly excluded from public life, as the leading Liberals were in the British election of 1918, and the Labour leaders in the election of 1931. In the fifth place, while political parties have their necessary function, and ought to be secure of representation proportionate to their strength, they ought not so completely to dominate elections and to define their issues as they now do in all countries.

The system of Proportional Representation, as it exists in most of the countries of continental Europe, secures the first of these objects, for every vote counts; in some degree it also secures the second, for all bodies of opinion are proportionally represented, in so far as they are expressed by the caucuses of organised parties. But it fails to secure the remaining objects; on the contrary, it accentuates instead of diminishing the power of party machines, and therefore discourages the election of men of independent minds and of inconveniently powerful intelligence. On the other hand, the use of what is known as " the single transferable vote " in large constituencies with several members meets all the requirements we have laid down.[1] It would not, of course, destroy the influence of political parties, which are essential to the working of democracy; but it would make them less rigid and more elastic and weaken the excessive control which they now

[1] The subject is fully discussed in my book, *How Britain is Governed* (Constable).

wield over their candidates and members, while it would encourage the most valuable of their activities, that of political education, by ensuring that the vote of every convert would count.

Under such a system elections would never produce the exaggerated " swings of the pendulum " to which we have become accustomed in Britain, or the violent oscillations of national policy which result from them; there would be a greater continuity both of personnel and of policy than the present system renders possible. In such a country as Britain neither violent revolution nor violent reaction will ever be supported by the nation as a whole. Either would be possible under the existing system; neither would be possible under the system we are discussing. It is probable that under such a system no single party would ever obtain a clear majority, or be able to wield dictatorial power; consequently Parliament would resume something of its old authority, the dictatorship of the Cabinet and the party caucus would be qualified, discussion would once more become real, and politicians would be compelled to aim at the greatest common measure of agreement. The value of such a change in the vital sphere of international relations can scarcely be over-estimated.

It is precisely these features and consequences of a genuinely representative system that arouse against it the opposition of party organisers; because they are loth to abandon the hope of obtaining for their party proposals a majority in Parliament without having to win over a majority in the country. They argue that Parliament would become unworkable if it really reflected the various bodies of opinion in the country; which is as much as to say that representative government is only practicable provided that it is *not* representative. They argue that "stable government" in a parliamentary system is only possible if one party commands a disciplined majority and is able to do exactly what it likes; which is as much as to say that the supremacy of Parliament is only tolerable if Parliament is not allowed to be supreme. In short, this theory maintains that democracy is only possible if it is reduced to futility, and made the means of bringing about violent oscillations in national policy which do not correspond with the nation's will, and which must have unhealthy effects.

There are other methods which would usefully contribute to purify the working of democracy without affecting its essential character. One of these would be the compulsory publication of the accounts of party funds, duly audited. Another would be the assumption by the State of a larger proportion of the cost of electioneering, combined with a stricter testing of the amounts spent by party organisations in this way: these changes would diminish the dependence of parties upon money contributions. Yet another would be the prohibition of the use, by party organisations, of vehicles to bring voters to the poll: those who will not vote unless they are fetched had better stay away. But none of these changes would materially weaken the dominating influence of party organisations in the democratic system; nor within wide limits is it desirable to do so. Party organisations are invaluable as instruments of political education; they are mischievous only when they are used to drive to the poll herds of voters who have no interest in, and no knowledge of, the subjects upon which they are made to express a judgment.

It is sometimes urged that, in view of the momentous importance, complexity and delicacy of the problems of foreign policy, these should be kept out of the arena of party controversy as far as possible: for these reasons international questions are largely withheld from frank discussion in Parliament. There is a good deal to be said for this view; and the writer has elsewhere [1] suggested a means whereby the necessary secrecy could be combined with a reasonable degree of consultation and the maintenance of continuity.

But it is useless to suggest that international problems can be wholly withdrawn from public discussion. Now, more fully than ever before, they have become the supreme issues upon which both the safety and the well-being of every people depend; and the attitude which a country's government ought to adopt upon peace and disarmament, upon trade relations with other countries, upon international debts and international monetary relations, has come to be of far more vital importance than its attitude upon purely domestic questions. These issues already are, and must continue to be, the main preoccupation of intelligent electors in all countries; and if democracy is to be safe for the world in the crisis of human history through

[1] *How Britain is Governed*, p. 242.

which we are passing, it is essential to secure, not that the democratic electorates shall be excluded from the consideration of these issues, but that the debate upon them shall be intelligently conducted.

The most important line of political cleavage in all countries is the cleavage between those who recognise and accept the political and economic interdependence of all nations and are prepared to base their whole policy upon the acceptance of this dominating fact; and, on the other hand, those who cling to the nationalist view and still hanker after the unattainable end of military and economic self-sufficiency, whether on the scale of the nation or on the scale of the Empire. According as the predominant opinion in the leading nations takes one side or the other in this vital debate, the world will be led towards an era of diffused prosperity and secure peace or driven into immitigable disaster. Here is a conflict over the very soul and destiny of humanity more profound and momentous than any conflict that has ever hitherto been staged in human history; and, in a very vague and confused way, it is being fought not merely in the conferences of statesmen, but in the debates of every democratic people.

Unfortunately for the clear discussion of these supreme issues, the main cleavage is crossed and confused by many other cleavages. In particular, those who take the international view are every-where deeply divided among themselves on other issues, and are drawn into sympathy on one point or another with some of those who take the nationalist view. In some countries there are both nationalist and internationalist clericals, and both nationalist and internationalist anti-clericals; in other countries there are both nationalists and internationalists who advocate a policy of restriction and rigid economy, and both nationalists and internationalists who favour a policy of expansion and courageous expenditure. Though Conservatives everywhere are predominantly nationalist, there are enlightened internationalists among them; and though Radicals everywhere are predominantly internationalist in sympathy, among them are to be found many vehement nationalists.

In short, the new and great issue cuts across party lines of division in every country; and electoral contests fought upon rigid party lines are very likely to produce results that will not correspond with the real opinions of the people on the supreme issue upon which the fate of the world depends. Here lies the greatest danger of party-dominated democracy.

It is sometimes urged that, in all countries, those who appreciate the greatest issue of our time should draw together and form a united force to resist the dangerous and exaggerated nationalism that is ruining the world. But this is an impracticable proposal, because the cross-cleavages among them are too serious to make effective co-operation possible. The only means of escape from this dilemma is to be found in a more elastic political system, less dominated by party disciplines, than any democratic country has yet been able to devise: an electoral system which will reflect far more subtly than is now possible the varied shades and combinations of public opinion, and which will reduce the dangerous power now wielded by the irresponsible voters who can be carried off their feet by panics, appeals to false patriotism, and crude bribes; a parliamentary system which will greatly modify the present dictatorship of the Cabinet and the party caucus, and make free discussion and cross-voting possible.

In the midst of a great crisis of human history, democracy is on its trial. If it cannot be purified of its defects, if it cannot be made the means of giving to the nations the leadership they need, its irresponsibility, its short-sighted partisan fanaticism, and its violent oscillations, which seldom correspond to the real movements of opinion, may bring our civilisation to ruin. If this should happen, it will not be because democracy as such has failed, but because it has not been equipped with the mechanism that might enable it intelligently to grapple with its tremendous responsibilities.